BUSINESS
Wisdom

STRATEGIES FOR
SUCCESS

First published: 2023 - Business Wisdom: Strategies for Success

ISBN 978-0-6457416-3-6

To Linda, Miss C and my editor Cassandra Charlesworth,
whose support and forbearance
make possible the finished work.

About the Author

Clive Enever is a renowned business strategist known for his expertise in the field of business management and leadership. With over 25 years of experience helping businesses of all sizes and industries achieve their goals, Clive has become a trusted advisor to many entrepreneurs and executives around the world.

By helping his clients discover clarity and develop strategies that facilitate easier engagement with their ideal clients, Clive enables them to achieve their business goals more effectively and consistently.

With *Business Wisdom: Strategies for Success,* readers can tap into Clive's wealth of wisdom and experience and apply it to their own business endeavours.

Clive's passion for business and his commitment to helping others succeed have been the driving force behind his successful career. As a business coach, Clive Enever helps entrepreneurs achieve the elusive work-life balance that includes financial success.

Guiding his clients in setting and working towards their goals, Clive's approach to coaching is focused on empowering his clients to achieve a fulfilling and successful business that aligns with their personal needs, values and aspirations.

Contents

Introduction

Why not?

"Some see things as they are and ask why. Others dream of things that never were and ask why not?"
George Bernard Shaw.

Call it entrepreneurship, small business, or working for yourself—running your own business revolves around the question 'why not?'

Why not take the plunge, go it alone, be your own boss, step outside your comfort zone, or challenge the status quo?

Why not dream big, start small, do it better, do it differently and march to the beat of your own drum?

Why not set the benchmark, be the rule maker, become the employer and relish the opportunity to be master of your own domain?

If the "why not" that accompanies starting your own business sounds familiar, then why not seize the opportunity to create a business that achieves all you hope for and more?

Business ownership can be immensely rewarding, infinitely liberating, and ultimately satisfying.

It can also be tough. It can be challenging to see the year ahead for the graft of the day to come.

It can be all-consuming and occasionally disheartening. And it's not a path you tread alone.

Within the pages of this book, we explore some of the common themes of being in business, addressing the why, asking why not, and looking to the potential road ahead.

The advice and guidance is provided in the knowledge that each business is as unique as the person who runs it. But often an enterprise will be faced with common challenges and themes.

What you take from the pages ahead depends upon what is applicable to you and your business story.

But never forget the passion that stirred you to embark on the business journey - continue to ask the question that saw you embrace entrepreneurship in the first place and use it to drive you forward.

Could you be better, is there room for growth, is there the chance to see things differently?

Do you continue to dream things that never were, and ask why not?

Chapter 1 - Being in Business

Being in business is no small achievement. It takes imagination, vision, and commitment to step outside the comfort zone and go it alone, with your own idea and ambition front of mind.

It requires bravery, resilience, innovation and an ability to see the big picture.

Ultimately, the rewards that come with backing yourself, taking the risk and having faith in your own vision can be immense.

Being in business can allow you to attain the lifestyle you deserve, enjoy the success you crave, and achieve the personal goals you set.

But for some, success is achieved faster than others, and it begs the question, what exactly is the recipe for business success?

The ingredients of success

From the outside it may seem that every business has a different recipe for their success.

But the reality is, there are key elements which every successful business shares - regardless of whether they are a tyre shop, a bakery or an industry-leading corporate communications brand.

So what constitutes success, and what are the major drivers behind it?

Dream

Describe it as dreaming or note it as goal setting, successful businesses have the ability to look to the future and consider where they want to go.

For some business owners that goal will be financial, for others it's about lifestyle, and for others still it's about market share or domination.

But regardless of the goal, it's about determining an achievable outcome in the future.

Plan

Dreams and goals are just words without planning to fulfil them. And this is where every successful business has some kind of plan to get where they want to go.

In small business it's that vital document, the "business plan". For corporations it's the "strategic plan", but this critical piece of paperwork is the blueprint to achieving goals. It sets out and crystallises who you are as a business, where you are and where you want to be, giving it clarity and achievability.

Enact

While a business plan is the overarching document that sets goals for your business, the strategies it engages are the paths to get there. And every successful business identifies the routes they will take to get to their destination.

These are the systems and procedures that will take you where you want to go - the "how-to" behind the "what" and the "where".

Involve

A business is only as successful as the people within it, which means great staff are a key ingredient to business success.

But they must also be given the tools to fulfil their job role and tackle any challenges, and this is done via communication and involvement.

Successful businesses share their vision with their staff, communicating where they plan to go and how the strategies and procedures will take them there.

Involvement is not just about staffing, however. It's about utilising the right people to help steer a business at the right time.

Successful businesses know when to call in the experts to help out, and they're not afraid to do so – whether that's an accountant, a lawyer, recruitment firm, the bank manager, or business coach or mentor.

Revise

Goals, dreams and plans shift over time, and it's important they are revisited regularly to gauge progress and to change tack if necessary.

This is done by measuring outcomes against your business plan and procedures, then revising the destination, route and strategies to incorporate new outcomes.

That revision may be based on changes in your industry, changes in technology or just changes in your ultimate destination. But regardless, it's a realisation that business is a living entity which will evolve over time.

The challenge of modern business

It's no secret modern business comes with both incredible opportunity and its own unique challenges.

On the one hand, the rise of the internet means it's never been easier to start a business.

On the other, it's never been more challenging to maintain and grow your business in a climate of new competition and innovation.

But how do you adapt to the challenge and opportunity of modern business?

Well, it all comes down to recognising the risks and handling them accordingly.

So let's delve into five of the biggest challenges in modern business and how you can address them...

Image

In an era where a business can be made or broken via online reviews and internet presence, never before has maintaining an image been so important.

Your image (whether it's honesty and integrity, speed and customer service, or prestige and professionalism) should be reflected in every aspect of your business.

This includes the staff you hire, the emails you send, the branding you embrace and the publicity you seek.

Throughout day-to-day business operations, expansion and new product considerations, a business owner should be asking themselves: "Does this (email, staff member, product, logo, website etc) reflect our core values and the way we want to be seen?"

Staffing

Again and again we hear it's the people who make a business. At a time where employees are increasingly mobile, the true art is attracting and keeping the right ones.

Every business should value their employees and furnish them with the right tools to excel at their jobs.

These include training, mentoring, clear systems and procedures, and recognising a job well done.

A happy workplace attracts great staff, but most importantly it keeps them.

Increased competition

With online businesses starting all the time and an emerging culture where small business is actively encouraged, new competition is one of the biggest challenges for existing business.

That means business owners should have their ear to the ground for potential competitors but most importantly should be proactive in their business activities.

This proactive approach is about ensuring the highest standards of business and customer service are maintained, while monitoring new innovations and evolving to suit the climate.

Marketing and customer loyalty

In line with increased competition, retaining customers who are loyal to your business is imperative.

And with so many businesses vying to get consumers' attention how do you get your particular message heard?

Fortunately social media and the digital age have opened up new rivers of marketing opportunity, but it's how a business uses them in a way that represents their image that counts.

This makes marketing and consumer loyalty strategies critical to modern business success.

Cash and resources

Creating and managing adequate streams of income to fund stability and growth is no new thing to business, but it remains one of the greatest challenges.

The best way to tackle it is through comprehensive planning. While a business may be easy to establish, without a plan it runs the risk of stagnating and failing within the first few years of operation.

Along the way the business should be consistently asking itself what it is, where it seeks to go and a whole host of other questions that shape its future and its customer experience.

The most important questions in business

When it comes to business, too often business owners become bogged down in the day-to-day running of things.

We get caught up in the operation and fail to look at the big picture of what we hope to achieve and how.

Success can be whittled down to a number of factors by answering some pertinent questions.

These are the questions a business owner should be asking in order to achieve success.

To really knock business right out of the park you need to know the answer to three critical things:

1. WHAT: Exactly WHAT you want to achieve

When we talk about going into business or shifting a business up a level, it's imperative to have a clear picture of what that business owner wants to achieve.

Whether it's a push to take a product from a stall at the market to supplying to retailers, a bid to go national, or a dream to bring a new service or product to the public, the WHAT is the core factor of business.

2. WHY: Why do you wish to bring your business product or service to the public?

When you know WHY, then you have passion and drive, which inspires massive and consistent action.

Business might be a labour of love, but it does not have to be a passion without economic reward.

Answering why you wish to start your business, build your business, or be in business; and why you wish for people to use this service or product is how you get to the galvanising core of your drive to achieve success.

3. HOW: How do you plan to achieve your goals?

Possibly the most important factor in achieving business success is having a plan of action for HOW success will be achieved and when.

Most people know WHAT they want to achieve and WHY, however far too many don't know HOW, and this is the essence of business planning and why it's so important.

The big question

Marketing pioneer Lester Wunderman famously noted: "The most dangerous question a prospect or customer asks is 'Why should I?' And they may ask it more than once..."

As a business owner you must know the answer to that question in order to provide the rational and emotional answers that inspire your customer to use your services, your products and your business.

And just an aside - if someone asks you that question, you have missed a fundamental part of engaging with a prospective customer. You have not discovered that the prospect has an interest in your product or service.

Answers bring clarity

Once you know WHAT you want, WHY you want it, HOW to get it and HOW to inspire your customers to use you, your path to business success is clear.

It's then important to note that every business has stages, and understanding where you are on that business timeline helps you embrace the challenges and successes that lie ahead.

Most common reasons businesses fail

Over the years there's been a lot of discussion about the grim statistics of businesses which fail, particularly in that first year.

You've probably heard them: one out of two, eight out of 10, and so on.

In actual fact research by analytics and data firm Veda that was published in the *Sydney Morning Herald*[1] indicates it's just 1.5 per cent that don't make it through to their first anniversary.

Instead, it's the first four years that count. It is the times when businesses have "to be brave and grow".

But to put that into context, many business owners can avert the risk of failure, simply by understanding where the common weak spots of enterprise are.

So here are five reasons businesses fail and what you can do to avoid it...

Inflexible planning

Business planning isn't something that ends with the first draft of strategies, market research and financial projections.

Over time businesses evolve from what they started out as to what they become. And chances are this evolution extends right throughout the life of an enterprise.

Later in this book we will take a deep dive into business planning, but it's important to understand from the outset, a well-written plan recognises an enterprise will change.

Indeed, a good plan identifies that potential growth and the changes that come with it.

Like the actual business, a plan should evolve in a proactive manner, recognising what will cause your successes, identifying what can bring failures and then directing the business accordingly. It's a living document that needs re-visiting, to ensure you are focussed on the right path over time.

Failure to communicate

Many a business has a great product, excellent staff and fabulous premises but that means nothing without communication and interaction with your customers.

Business is about feedback and promotion: knowing what the consumer wants and telling them you have it.

This applies in so many ways that it's list-worthy, so here we go...

If you're in business you should:

- ◆ Seek feedback and referrals
- ◆ Have an online presence
- ◆ Have a marketing plan
- ◆ Have an advertising strategy
- ◆ Be actively looking for incoming technology, trends and new ideas
- ◆ Keep an eye on prospective and actual competition

The best way to manage this is through two-way

communication with your clientele.

Poor cash management

So, you've defied the perceived odds and made it through the first year. Excellent…what about the next three?

How do you fund expansion, deal with recession, offer more, or handle additional staff and production?

How do you keep a rein on your finances, ensuring sufficient cashflow at any given moment in time?

In fact, lack of sufficient cashflow is one of the key reasons that a business may fail, and avoiding this situation comes down to the simple things like policies for accounts receivable, timely invoicing, working with the right customer and more.

At a higher level, it involves keeping track of the numbers of your business, having them on hand and on paper, while planning for the additional outlays that may come with expansion.

Meanwhile, somewhere along the line every business hits the sweet spot where they've been through the good and the bad and know exactly what cash and resources they need on hand.

Having arrived at this point, a business owner may also decide they understand what's going on and relax.

Whilst finding your comfort zone in business is important, it's worth being mindful that just because you've achieved a particular point in the journey doesn't mean there is no longer a need to keep your finger on the pulse and also plan for the future.

Lack of mobility

A great initial idea is only the beginning of business, after that it's about identifying 'your' market and adapting to any changes within it.

Many a successful business has sunk after years in the industry because they were too set in their ways to embrace mobility; to see what might be on the horizon and change tack accordingly.

It's about "bravery and growth" or being willing to embrace the entrepreneurial spirit and take a calculated risk.

Inefficient management

You might have had the idea, you might have provided the initial capital, but are you the best person to lead this team?

Or is there someone better for the role at a different time?

Management not only dictates the direction of a company but the ethos and morale within it. Good management will look within and outside a business for inspiration and direction. It will operate with clinical efficiency, passion and zeal.

That means, to ensure business success, you may need the humility to step aside and bring in fresh resources when you're outside your comfort zone or the battle of business sees you fatigued.

The beauty of business

The beauty of business is that it's about independence, creativity and lifestyle. But there's no one-way ticket out of hard work, passion and endurance.

By knowing the risks, the course to take to counter them and by remaining vigilant and nimble, business can take you to heights you never dreamed of and allow you to enjoy the satisfaction you deserve.

The secret seven

Just as there are common reasons that businesses fail, there are also common issues that businesses face, regardless of what industry or sector they represent.

Often these issues are the early warning signs of a greater struggle that may later see the business at risk.

So, let's examine the seven most common issues in business.

Too few clients

Whether it's too few clients or too few of the right clients, knowing who you are selling to, or providing a service for, is critical to success in business.

Too often business owners fail to direct their energy at the right area and miss an opportunity to market to and attract the clients who will ensure their business success.

Poor communication

How are you communicating with your potential clients and where? Effective communication and networking means talking to the right people at the right time in the right way.

Good communication equals happier customers and more sales.

Too long at work

Many of us fall into the trap of spending too much time working in our business without achieving the desired result.

If you know what you want to achieve, can identify the best person to achieve that outcome and understand how that works into the bigger picture of your business success, it will allow you to spend less time behind your desk and more time enjoying your life.

People management

Failing to manage and communicate with your staff effectively is a critical and common mistake in business.

By delegating tasks to the right people at the right time, employing the right person for the job, and implementing the procedures and processes that allow them to do that job, you allow for better employee relations, fewer employees and ultimately can reduce your overheads.

Lack of clarity

It's easy to get lost in the day-to-day running of a business and fail to see the bigger picture of what you are hoping to achieve.

If you can decide where you want to go, the goals you want to achieve and, most importantly, how you are going to get there, you can get on with the job of running your business with the knowledge it is getting ahead.

Not enough sales

Seems obvious doesn't it, but this one takes some thought. If you're not making enough sales why is that the case?

Consider:

- ◆ **The profit drivers:** Are you marketing your product to the right people? In other words, who is your ideal client? And how do you get more of them? What are the critical steps in your marketing, sales or other processes that affect profit? What needs to improve?

- ◆ **Enquiries:** Where do they come from? How many are they? What are they? How can you drive the right type of enquiry?

- ◆ **Your sales pipeline:** What does it look like? Does it leak? Where and why? What effect does your activity have on this? Is it positive/negative?

Not enough money

As mentioned earlier, cashflow is critical to business success and the answer to gaining more money from your business will likely be somewhere within the factors above.

If you increase your sales, reduce your overheads, and know what you want to achieve, the monetary results will speak for themselves.

Key takeaway: The pitfalls of business may be numerous and there may be more than one problem within a single business but the the solutions are plentiful too and they can be easily implemented and achieved.

Working 'on', not just 'in' your business

One of the biggest mistakes most business operators make is to get so caught up in the day-to-day operation of an enterprise that they fail to work on, not just in their business.

This leads to being reactive rather than proactive. As a result, plans and dreams are forgotten and doing the day-to-day takes precedence to the extent that suddenly you are just fixing issues - not running a business.

So how do you shift the focus? Well it's about prioritising, keeping the big picture in mind, and knowing when to delegate tasks to other staff members or an external person.

Let's delve a little deeper...

Make time

Every business owner should be setting aside a specific block of time to work on their business – whether that involves looking at the figures, setting goals, planning or revising policy.

In theory that sounds easy, but as any business operator will tell you, this time often falls by the wayside when other, more immediate "dollar productive" tasks pop up.

In other words, it's easy to defer going through your figures when the opportunity to quote on a new project or actually complete a job arises.

The important thing to remember here is that working on your business builds income for the long run, positioning you where you want to be in the future, while working in your business meets an immediate need right now.

So how do you resolve these two opposing business elements?

First think of this: Why did you start your own business?

Typical answers usually refine down to having time to do the things you want, whenever you want, wherever you want.

Ironically, often the first thing to go when a person starts a business is time.

Without a considered and detailed plan, time is easily lost.

Many people think that the time taken to plan is just a waste. Yet people with a well- researched and well-written plan are the ones with less going wrong, more going right and they also have the money to do the things they want. They also regain time.

It is often said that 10 minutes planning will save two hours in the doing.

Over the years I've seen a few hours of detailed strategic planning change a business from years of frustration, worry, stress and angst to a business delivering on its goals and objectives seemingly overnight.

Consider it an investment

Although it might be hard to quantify in dollar terms, it's critical to recognise that planning, revising and preparing are actually income producing tasks – you just don't tend to see the results immediately.

While the results might not be instantly apparent, clear and detailed planning followed by working the plan creates the environment for the delivery of results time and time again.

Recognise that planning is an investment in your business, so factor it into your business costs and allocate sufficient time within the working week when you essentially pay yourself for your expert business insight.

Delegate

If you're finding you do not have the time to work on your business due to interruptions or the fact you are on the job, it's time to look at delegating the more menial tasks during set periods.

Is there someone else in your business who could handle incoming phone calls for an hour? Could you outsource the invoicing? Is there software that might make your work more efficient so you have a little time to spare?

Make it part of your routine

Whether it's Friday afternoon or first thing Monday morning, block time in your calendar and stick to it.

This is a period when you are unavailable to take calls, answer emails, schedule meetings or see staff. Unless it is an emergency, this block of time is non-negotiable.

Remember, it doesn't have to be a lengthy period. Even just an hour a week starts to add up when it comes to working on where you want your business to go.

Have your files and notes accessible

There's no point spending half of your allotted planning time seeking out the documents you need and looking for notes you have previously taken.

Have a dedicated folder, drawer, shelf or file where your business planning information resides. Keep this information separate from other tasks so you can easily come back to it and pick up where you left off previously.

Key takeaway: Working on your business allows it to build momentum over time. It enables you to chart where you want to go personally and professionally then set goals and meet them.

It's about the big-picture not the fine print, and when you keep that front of mind, and make working on your business a habit, you will find you have greater clarity and an improved ability to take your business where you want it to go.

Chapter 2 - Planning

It doesn't matter if your business is in the start-up phase, five years old or a second generation enterprise, planning plays a critical role throughout the life of every business.

If you're not planning, you are not moving forward, you are not enjoying growth, you are not realising your business potential, and you are certainly not preparing to avoid the worst.

The value of a plan

Planning looks at where your business is now and identifies opportunities available to it.

It lays the foundations through goal setting, encapsulates your business vision, allows you to examine your strengths, weaknesses, opportunities and threats, and ensures you create a roadmap for your business moving forward.

Most importantly, good planning identifies your ideal client in the knowledge this is the person your business is talking to, serving and seeking to satisfy.

When to look at your plan

The reality is every business should take a good, hard look at their business plan each year, examining whether they are actually doing what the plan shows.

If not, what needs to change? Is the plan wrong or is the business other than what you wanted it to be when you started?

If the plan aligns with the outcomes you want, then look at your activity.

If the activity aligns with what the business is about, then look at your planning. Have you met previous goals? How did they shape up compared to the proposed plan?

Now, where do you intend to go from here?

The details of business can change a lot in the year, and there's never been a better time than now to reassess your performance and plan for the future.

The art of planning

Ultimately, all planning activities will be documented in your all-important business plan, but the process starts long before that with the vision for your business, along with brainstorming, goal setting and measuring business activity.

Then, each of these is formalised as part of your business plan.

Vision

Every business plan ties back to the vision for an enterprise. It takes in what the business hopes to achieve in the short-term, and incorporates the steps that bring that vision to life.

While a vision is about the 'what', the plan is about the 'how', looking at the position of the business now and what needs to be achieved for that vision to come to fruition.

We shall take a deep-dive into how you formulate a Vision statement in the next chapter, but suffice to say, it is one of the key foundations of any plan.

The power of brainstorming in business

We all know the value of planning and creating clear, actionable, and achievable goals for business.

But long before those goals and ideas become enshrined in your business plan, they need to be proposed, tested, proved and prioritised.

One of the most powerful tools for this task is brainstorming.

So let's talk a little about ideas generation through brainstorming, and the best ways of translating the random concept into the real plan for business.

Brainstorming

Brainstorming forms the basis of the goals and plans that your business hopes to attain.

As the Australian Institute of Business[2] explains, brainstorming is: "the mulling over of ideas by one or more individuals in an attempt to devise or find a solution to a problem".

And in business it holds incredible value. Effective brainstorming allows a team or individual to think laterally, creatively and quickly, with one idea often leading to another.

Not only does brainstorming solve problems or hone concepts, it can also serve to bring a workplace together to take joint responsibility for the future, which in turn has very real benefits for morale.

The rules of brainstorming

Rules, what rules? The beauty of brainstorming is there aren't any, but there are some useful tools and aids to help the process flow more smoothly...

Set aside sufficient time

Whether you're brainstorming independently or pulling your team together to discuss a matter, ensure sufficient time is devoted to the task. This should be a block of time without interruption in a space suited to your business environment.

Bear in mind 'sufficient' isn't overly lengthy. Ideally a brainstorming session will take about 30 minutes, but could feasibly be as little as 15 or as much as 45. Anywhere beyond that and people start to lose their enthusiasm.

Assign a leader

A brainstorming session is best guided by a group leader, whose role involves keeping the creative juices flowing, while ensuring the team doesn't get sidetracked.

No idea is off the table

By nature, brainstorming is a process that should encourage lateral thinking. That means the environment should be non-judgmental and 'safe'.

Sometimes the ideas that come from left of field prove to have real merits, so encourage your staff to set aside their egos and self-consciousness, and say exactly what they think.

This is not the time for evaluation

On that note, the brainstorming session is not the time for evaluation. That comes later, so don't let the group get hijacked by weighing the pros and cons of a concept.

Editing a thought or idea at its inception is akin to killing it before it has drawn breath. Editing it is trying to fit it into what you know now. The beneficial outcome here is to give it legs, let it run. Let it prove its worth.

While you might later prove the idea does not have merit, you might learn something which will allow your business to grow in ways and at speed you did not previously believe were possible.

Brainstorming is building

The reason brainstorming works so well is that one idea often forms the foundation for another. That's why it's particularly effective in a group situation.

Someone might offer a perspective or idea no-one else had thought of and the ideas begin to grow from there. The original idea might lack value. The ideas conceived because of the original might be the goldmine.

Write it large

Brainstorming is a verbal and visual activity, so when those ideas start erupting, write them big and bold.

Where to from here?

Once you have completed your brainstorming session, let it sit a little before evaluation. It's often useful to bring an alternative team in for the evaluation session to offer a fresh set of eyes.

Then take the standout ideas and set them as goals or actionable plans. Once those goals have been established, you can begin working back through the steps and timeframe required when it comes to achieving that goal.

Goal setting - Get SMART

Whether you've brainstormed potential ideas or have some specific goals for your business, the key milestones you intend to achieve are critical to business planning.

The reality is goals come in all shapes and forms - sales targets, growth expectations, proposed machinery acquisition, performance goals for staff, and what about something for you? - some time off perhaps.

These goals are key to the future direction of an enterprise, but they're not just arbitrary wishes that business owners cast out to the universe with their fingers crossed that dreams might come true.

Effective goal setting involves being very clear about what you want to do, with a timeframe in mind and measurements in place to ensure you get where you intend to go.

Since the 1980s this outcome-driven goal setting has been known as SMART, and it's one of the most popular and effective means of setting realistic goals that a business can actively achieve.

Here's how SMART goal setting works, and how you can employ its power...

SMART goal setting

Coined in the early '80s as a management tool, the term SMART is a simple acronym to ensure goals are specific, measurable, attainable, realistic, and timely.

It allows a business to give goals actionable clarity, a time frame and measure progress during implementation.

Importantly SMART goal setting allows a business to think through its objectives considering what, who, why, how, and when.

Here's a quick guide to the elements and what they cover...

Specific - Goals may be based on dreams but they need to be specific to be actionable and this involves considering the who, what, when, which and why behind their application.

In other words, who or what will contribute to achieving an outcome, why are you working towards this goal, which goal takes priority, and how and when will it occur?

Measurable - Business progress is best tracked through measurement, so all goals should have set criteria that enables you to ascertain whether a plan is working.

This allows you to revise the required actions, if necessary, in order to meet the objective.

Attainable - Establishing goals that are attainable involves considering how you will achieve an outcome and acquiring the attitudes, skills, abilities and procedures necessary to do so.

Realistic - Are your goals realistic? Nothing kills motivation quite as effectively as an unrealistic expectation that can never be met.

To ensure your goals are realistic you may need to establish milestones, actions and criteria to get you to a larger outcome in the future.

Timely - Goals should be bound to a specific timeframe to ensure they remain a priority and are enacted.

Even SMARTER

Over recent years some organisations have even gone a step further than just SMART goal setting, in a bid to make their objectives SMARTER.

In this instance, two further criteria are applied to the establishment of goals to ensure goals are Evaluated and Reviewed.

Evaluated - Set regular time periods to gauge how your goals are progressing or whether they remain an effective and relevant aim.

This involves analysing the measurements and ascertaining whether you are on track or need to revise your strategy to attain the outcome you desire.

Reviewed - Whether complete or still in progress, goals should be reviewed regularly.

This allows you to tick the box when a milestone has been met, set further objectives for future planning, or reassess the effectiveness of current strategies you have in place.

The relationship between goals and values

In both life and business, when it comes to setting goals they are not created in a vacuum. They should be viewed within the context of the values you espouse.

Why? Because when the goals align with the values, they are more achievable. They become the stepping stones supporting your journey that get you where you want to go.

So, let's delve a little deeper into the relationship between goals and values, and how you can ensure they align.

Values and goals – a definition

Values - Put simply, values are what we stand for. They are what guide our decision making on our inevitable direction as we move throughout life and business.

Often these values are incorporated within the Vision and Mission statements that we create for a business, but they are not necessarily one and the same.

Goals – On the other hand, goals are what we want to see happen and what we aspire to achieve. They are the milestones we need to reach on the journey of business and life. They are the given points of achievement delivering desired outcomes and cause for celebration.

Goals are not idle wishlists that we cast into the ether, they are milestones that we then apply actions to in a bid to ensure they are met.

The process

In business we look at goals from the perspective of the entre-preneur's personal values, the business' values and the vision and mission of what you ultimately hope to achieve.

That means when setting goals we often ask questions that span both the personal and the professional, like:

- ◆ What are your top three goals in life right now?
- ◆ What are your five most important values?
- ◆ What is your favourite thing to do? (that gives you the most personal satisfaction)
- ◆ What would you be doing if you were NOT worried about money?
- ◆ What have you always wanted to do but for whatever reason, failed to try?
- ◆ What would you do if there was no fear of failing? (I.e. You could not fail)

When we look at goals within the context of values, we can ensure they are achievable and work to take a business in the direction and to the destination you want to go.

Turning goals into actions

Setting goals is not the end of the process. We then need to make them actionable habits that can be achieved.

To do this we need to write those goals down and plan exactly the process required to attain them.

At this stage it's also useful to assess whether our goals are

SMART – as in specific, measurable, actionable, realistic and timely.

This process of assessing our goals, writing them down, then measuring and evaluating progress allows us to form good habits, in the knowledge the actions we repeat time and again add up to get us where we want to go.

As the saying goes, "persistence overcomes resistance".

Simple steps to setting goals

We know goals are important. Given they are vitally important, why do we so often fail to achieve goals?

Typically this is because we don't clearly establish our goal in the first place, or we don't plan the steps required to achieve the goal.

Like every process, using a goal setting system encourages you to think about the whole journey, factoring in the thinking, deciding, planning, activity, measuring, and achievement.

Start with the thinking

♦ **What do you want to achieve/have/be?**

Work through this process to dispense with the things which simply feel good just now and identify the goal that you really want.

To identify what you really want, consider who you will 'be' upon achieving this goal.

Is that the person you want to be? Will being that person satisfy you? Does the thought of achieving this goal inspire you? If it doesn't inspire you, there is a high likelihood that you will not work to achieve the goal.

Decide upon your goal because you will value achieving it.

◆ **Be sure your goal fits the SMART criteria**

Specific – What, who, when, where, how, why?
Measurable – Create criteria and/or KPIs to track your progress.
Attainable – Develop attitudes, abilities, skills. Plan your steps.
Realistic – Ensure you are willing and able to work towards your goal.
Timely – Anchor your goal to a specific date.

Writing down your goals encourages you to focus and makes them more real, more tangible. It changes the goal from merely being a vague idea - which you can easily lose sight of when another idea appears - to being something you can refer to often to maintain your focus and your motivation.

◆ **Create an action plan**

Be precise. Identify the roles and tasks required. Determine how you will meet your goal. As you work through what activities are required you might find smaller goals that need to be achieved as part of the one journey. Identify these milestones as minor goals or objectives that need to be met as a measure of progress.

◆ **Create a timeline**

You know now what is required, now plan the timeline to maintain a sense of urgency and help with focus. Keep to the established times and your goal will be achieved.

- **Take action - Begin**

  Each step taken will lead to the next and the next until all steps are completed. And, upon completion, your goal will be achieved.

- **Monitor and evaluate progress**

  Monitor each activity and evaluate the result. If not enough has been done, increase the activity.

- **Celebrate success**

  Each win along the journey deserves to be celebrated, leading to a greater appreciation of achieving the goal.

Goal achievement flow chart

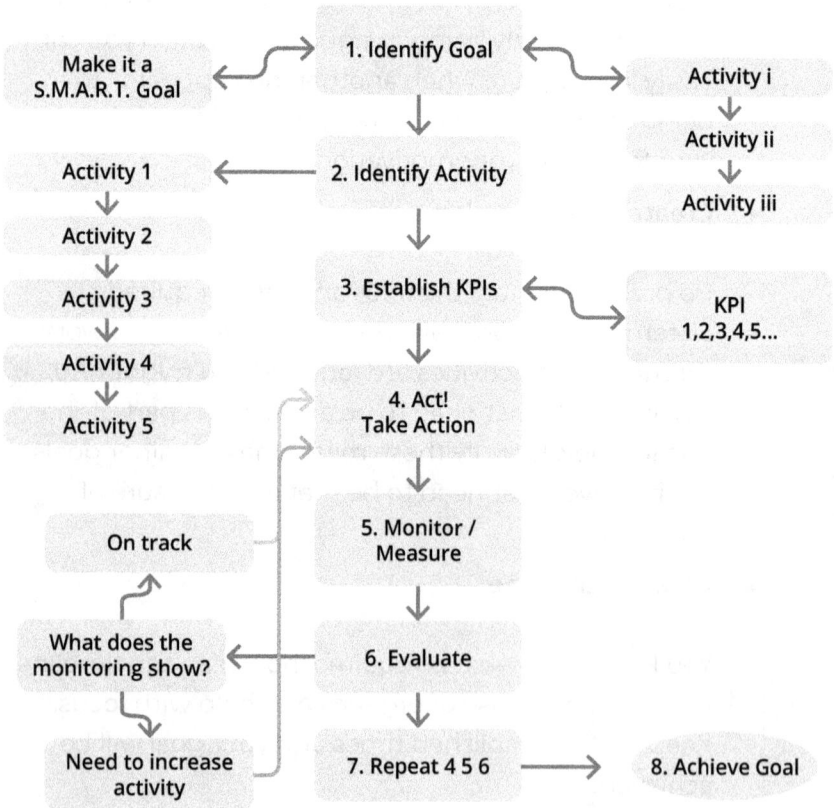

Make it a S.M.A.R.T. Goal	1. Identify Goal	Activity i → Activity ii → Activity iii
Activity 1 → Activity 2 → Activity 3 → Activity 4 → Activity 5	2. Identify Activity	
	3. Establish KPIs	KPI 1,2,3,4,5...
	4. Act! Take Action	
On track	5. Monitor / Measure	
What does the monitoring show?	6. Evaluate	
Need to increase activity	7. Repeat 4 5 6 → 8. Achieve Goal	

From goals to growth reality

Transforming your goals from dreams to reality requires action that involves planning, measuring and accountability. So, let's look at these three areas and how they form the bridge between a concept and a reality.

Planning

Once you have set a goal, you need to identify the steps required to enact it. That might entail hiring additional staff, sourcing additional products, or investment in extra equipment.

But the aim is to clearly identify exactly what you are looking to achieve and then work backwards, outlining all the small steps you need to take to make that goal happen.

This forms the road map and checklist of each individual action you need to take to enact that goal.

Checklists

The path from goal to reality is paved with checklists and at this point they are your best friend. Say for example, you have identified you wish to increase production of a product...

Your checklist might include:

1. Obtain quotes on additional equipment required
2. Investigate costs of equipment installation
3. Source a business loan or draw on available equity
4. Set timeframe for equipment installation
5. Prepare worksite for addition of equipment
6. Create enough product to see you through site downtime during installation
7. Hire additional staff for increased output
8. Distribute marketing to alert customers of increased product availability

Ultimately, checklists with set timeframes ensure you hold yourself accountable.

Measuring

In addition to establishing checklists, as a business you also need to measure what you're doing, and this usually takes the form of KPIs (key performance indicators).

KPIs help you answer the questions of business and identify when the time has come to take action.

In other words, they often act as triggers.

For example, what metric do you need to reach to know when you actually need to increase production of a product?

KPIs also help you measure success. So, when you implement that new equipment, the KPIs you reach ensure you understand that the investment in new equipment for increased production is paying off.

Like checklists, KPIs ensure you stay accountable. If you are not reaching your target figures it's an indicator something is not working and either the goal needs to be revised or the way you seek to achieve it needs to be changed. Ideally the goal is well set and therefore the activity will be adjusted, not the goal.

Accountability

In business, there are many ways to hold yourself accountable to your aims.

These include writing things down, incorporating them into your business plan, and openly sharing what you are looking to achieve.

You can also ensure you remain accountable by setting aside time each week to work on a specific goal.

The allocated time doesn't have to be huge but is designed to allow you to progressively achieve your aim.

Putting your current business in perspective

Your goals might be lofty and your plans for the future impressive, but they also need to be weighed against the current position of your business.

And that's where two of the most useful tools in business come into their own, allowing you to identify the strengths and weaknesses of your enterprise along with any threats.

Two valuable business tools - SWOT and Porter Five Forces

Any tool that can help you better understand your position, potential and possible problems in business can be valuable in terms of helping you set goals, create your business plan, achieve market share and identify areas of improvement.

So, let's take a quick walk through two of the most common tools that are utilised when starting a business and throughout the business journey.

SWOT

This is one of the most well-known strategies in business, and sees operators take a critical view of their enterprise to analyse its Strengths, Weaknesses, Opportunities and Threats.

SWOT is a technique used throughout the life of a business when planning and clarifies both internal and external factors that are favourable and unfavourable for achieving any objective.

Within this framework, strengths and weaknesses tend to be focussed on the internal workings of the business, while opportunities and threats look at the external environment.

SWOT ANALYSIS

	Helpful to achieving the objective	Harmful to achieving the objective
Internal Origin (attributes of the organisation)	Strenghts	Weaknesses
External Origin (attributes of the environment)	Opportunities	Threats

SWOT assessments work by seeing you list the following:

- Strengths - These are the characteristics of the business or project that give it an advantage over others.

- Weaknesses - These are the characteristics of the business that place the business or project at a disadvantage relative to others.

- Opportunities - Elements in the environment that the business or project could exploit to its advantage.

- Threats - Elements in the environment that could cause potential problems for the business or project.

Porter Five Forces

Created by Michael E Porter of Harvard University in 1979, Porter Five Forces is a tool for examining the competitive environment for business.

It's often used during start-up or when considering the viability of a new business, product line or service and when seeking to determine the price point of a product/service.

Porter Five looks at:

- Industry Rivalry - This seeks to understand the number and strength of your competitors. Where there are few competitors or they lack strength, you'll likely be able to command a high price and enjoy healthy profits.

- Threat of substitutes - This examines how likely it is that your customer will be able to find a slightly different service or product to meet the same need, or whether they can fulfil the service themselves.

- Bargaining power of buyers - In this instance you're asking what is the likelihood buyers can drive my price down? How many buyers are there, what's the value of their orders, can they go elsewhere, or dictate the price of your products?

- Threat of new entrants - How easy is it for new competitors to get a foot in the door of your sector? This examines areas like regulation and entry affordability. If it's easy and affordable for competitors to enter your market, you are likely to have more competition over time.

- Bargaining power of suppliers - This area looks at your relationship with suppliers.

  How many potential suppliers are there for the product or service you sell, what's the demand for them and the likelihood they can raise their prices?

It's important to appreciate that business is often a "work in progress", which benefits immensely from taking a step back to ascertain what's working, what's not and where there may be room for improvement or an untapped opportunity.

Both SWOT and Porter's Five offer this insight, providing a valuable big-picture perspective of where your business is now and where it has the opportunity to go.

Putting it all together - Your business plan...

A good business plan is like a map of where you want to go and what activities are required to ensure success.

It takes into account what issues or factors you are likely to encounter along the way and any additional learning you might require for your journey, given your expertise and experience in your chosen field.

With a good plan, a business owner gains clarity from the chaos of their dreams, wishes and desires, and with clarity comes the certainty of success.

Knowing how...

Most business owners know WHAT they want to do or achieve, they also have the passion and the knowledge WHY they want to do it, but far too many business owners don't know HOW to achieve their goals and business planning is all about the HOW.

The steps...

To create a proper business plan you need to work through a process:

1. Thoughts – These are your dreams, wishes and aspirations.

2. More thoughts - Research; Review; Analyse; Check; Scrutinise.

3. Chaos – The period between thoughts, dreams and action.

4. Form and direction – Work through the chaos to find form and direction.

5. Clarity – With the form and direction comes clarity.

6. Certainty – From clarity you can begin to act upon your dreams with certainty.

7. Success – Certainty about what you want and how to achieve it is success.

8. Activity – While we cannot control the result, we can control the activity.

9. Result – The activity determines the result.

The result…

With a proper business plan in hand so much more can open up to you, enabling you to be more certain and relaxed about your business. A plan allows you to be more comfortable and the clarity allows you to achieve more in less time. It will lead you to become a better employer with better employee relations.

A plan allows for reduced overheads, increased returns, and happier customers.

Importantly in this age where we struggle with work/life balance, it gives you more time for yourself and family and… more money.

A comprehensive plan is a plan for success.

Your business plan is where your vision, brainstorming, SMART goals, and SWOT assessment come together into a formal document that factors in each and maps the future for your business.

It's about envisaging your dream business and committing it to paper.

And it's important to remember, while the dream might be something from the future, what you are committing to paper is right now in the present.

This gives you a much greater opportunity to achieve the outcomes that you want, in a much shorter time span.

It's also important to remember, whatever your business does, it does for a particular customer, within a particular time, under particular circumstances and *it does it to please you*.

It works this way so that you can enjoy doing what you do for people you like to work with.

What your plan will cover:

- Analysis of the environment in which you propose to run this business
- The products or services which you will provide
- Your customer demographics
- The competition and, as a consequence of understanding the competition, your comparative advantage.
- A price strategy that explains why your prices are what they are.
- The advertising and promotion that will be required, including how this happens and how you will get the message out to your ideal customer.
- Your Strengths, Weaknesses, Opportunities and Threats [SWOT].

Detailed analysis of all the above will highlight the many, many things necessary to allow your business to be successful.

When you are commencing a business, a detailed business plan ensures you are starting from the right position to gain the right level of business activity, right from day 1.

When you have an existing business, working out what needs to change to make the business work is often a remedy for stress and anxiety along with the antidote for a business at risk of failure.

Of course there are things which change from time to time within a business. But a good plan will not need change for the time the business does what the business is set up to do.

For example, it's important to understand that whilst you might have results of X across a given period of time, you might very well want to do better in the next period of time.

This is goal setting and achievement. Goal setting, monitoring and subsequent achievement is not part of your business plan.

The plan identifies how the business operates, under what conditions the business operates, what the business provides by way of products or services and who the business provides those products and services to.

Goals and all things associated with them relate to the level of performance or how often the business does what the business does; how many times in a given period of time the business delivers what the business delivers.

Therefore it is not the business plan itself which requires change but the goals and objectives relating to the business performance.

The business itself doesn't change. The business, regardless of the goals and objectives, no matter how great they may be, does not change.

The business still does what the business does and has always done. What has changed is how often or how frequently within a given period of time the business does what the business does.

As a business grows and evolves, more staff might be required to perform either the same roles more often or to perform new roles created as a result of the growth of the business.

Often a business runs into trouble at this point in time. Often a business recognises a period of growth and therefore a need for a new role to be filled and in haste a decision is made to fill that role.

Just as with most other aspects of the business these roles can be identified before the business even begins, if a clear understanding of what outcomes can be achieved are identified and established as goals.

Therefore even before the business has begun the person required to fill a particular role is already identified, along with what skills are required to undertake the tasks required and what level of performance within the role is acceptable.

Identifying such criteria before the business has begun means that when the opportunity arrives to appoint a person to the role, the right person will be selected.   And indeed, rather than filling a role in haste, if the right person doesn't turn up at the first round of interviews, continue looking until the right person is discovered.

In other words, remember, writing a business plan which identifies what you have today rather than identifying what it is that you want to have as your business, means that you are making a plan to stay precisely where you are.

Your business plan

Your business plan is a living document that guides the direction of your enterprise throughout its lifespan.

As such, it is one of the most important documents that you have, and is a critical tool to guide your business' success.

What the plan is used for:

Starting a business

If you are starting a business, your business plan helps you turn your idea into a reality, looking at the current market, your planned position within it, your financing requirements and more.

It helps determine whether your goals and vision for a new venture are realistic, and allows you to understand the budget required.

Running a business

If you have an existing business, a regularly updated and reviewed business plan allows you to identify opportunities for growth and expansion, along with potential risks that may impact the business' viability.

It charts the ongoing direction of your business and provides clarity about the steps you need to take in order to achieve your aims.

Selling a business

If you are considering selling your business, a comprehensive business plan is an important tool to attract buyers.

It offers an insight into the business' potential, its value and its proposed direction.

The elements of a business plan

A business plan combines all the elements of a business in one neat document. It includes other plans that might stand alone, such as your marketing plan, vision, financial position and more.

Beginning - Key detail and executive summary

This section provides a snapshot of your business including key details like its physical address, business number, corporate structure, any licences required, and contact details.

The executive summary then outlines the proposed or existing concept for the business. It is often written once all other details of the plan have been finalised and provides a succinct overview of the business.

Part 1 - The marketing plan

The marketing plan defines the strategies you will use to reach your ideal customer, and how you will retain existing clientele.

This plan also draws on the previous marketing analysis, looking at who your ideal customer is, where you will reach them and how you will communicate with them.

Part 1.2 - Product or service market analysis

This section describes the services or products that you currently offer or intend to offer, along with your analysis of market demand for them.

It considers your strengths, opportunities, weaknesses and threats, and involves   researching your competition.

The analysis conducted in this section also helps you determine things like your ideal customer, your pricing strategy and point of difference.

Part 2 - The operating plan

The operating plan is one of the most important elements of the business plan, describing exactly how the business works.

It includes details on how your business products and services are provided, along with information about your business premises, equipment, any lease terms, labour, machinery, technology and environmental considerations.

Part 2.2 - Legal and risk management

This section of the plan is about identifying obligations and risks. It includes the licences and/or permits you require, the insurance you need, and defines any risks associated with your business.

The aim of this part of the plan is to outline potential risks and illustrate how you will mitigate them.

Part 3 - Management and personnel plan

The management and personnel plan looks at the staffing requirements of your business, including staff roles, job descriptions, human resources policies, and training.

It also determines the credentials required of your staff and helps you plan for the current and future staffing needs of your business.

Part 4 - Finance plan

This section of the business plan is all about the cold, hard numbers of your business, and looks at things like:

- Your break even point
- Projected cashflow
- Funding arrangements, including any loans and loan terms

This information is designed to protect you financially, giving you clear numbers that you need to achieve in order for your business to be viable then profitable.

It is critical this section is accurate and is a vital part of a business plan if you are seeking finance.

Annexure - The action plan

The action plan is all about your intended future for your business. In this section you define the tasks which need to be completed in order to achieve your goals, along with the timeframes it is anticipated these tasks will be completed within.

Any resources required to achieve your objectives should also be outlined in this section.

Scan the QR code below to access the Business Plan Template.

Download Template

10 things that make your business plan work

Whether you're looking for funding, setting up a business or examining growth, a business plan is one of the most vital documents you can invest your time and effort in creating.

It gives you the road map for where your business will go, what its potential is and the market you are competing within. Here are 10 things that make your business plan work.

The devil is in the detail

A business plan isn't worth the paper it's written on if the details aren't properly completed with adequate research.

Take the time to research the type of information that should be contained or seek professional assistance, then work through each section of the document and provide enough detail for the reader to make informed decisions about your business.

It's a living document

Any plan should be considered a living document. It will evolve, alter and change over time. That's why it's essential to revisit your business plan throughout the life of your business.

At a glance

One of the most important sections of any business plan is the summary. It should be written in a professional manner that briefly touches on the themes that will be revisited in more detail later in the document.

Basically it's an overview, so ensure it is brief enough to keep the reader's attention but honed enough to adequately capture the essential elements of your business.

Keep your audience in mind

There are a variety of reasons to write a business plan. It might be to attain initial or growth funding, to sell your business or to examine where your business is at and what the future has the potential to hold.

Whatever the reason, write the plan with an audience in mind.

Do the figures

The figures are arguably the most important element of your plan, and they are likely to be pored over in depth. Ensure your figures are up to date and accurate.

Know your market

For your own benefit and for that of others who are looking to your plan for guidance, you should know the market you operate within intimately.

Your plan should outline the demographic you target, including who the product or service is aimed at, the size of the market, their likely income and spending habits.

Consider your competition

Your business plan should also reference competition or potential competition as this affects your market share. It's about knowing who you're going up against.

Show the potential

Is there a segment of your market that's untapped? Is there a new product you could use or better technology that would allow you to increase revenue? Outline the potential of your business and what it could do based on these scenarios.

Do the projections

A business plan is not just about now, it's about the future, so it should include projected earnings and future revenue streams.

Refer to the plan

Once you have a plan, use it. This is a valuable document that should have revealed a path forward.

Utilising its recommendations, strategies and procedures, use it to finance, build or hone your business.

Making the most of your business plan

Creating a business plan is just the beginning. Once you have it you need to use it to achieve the outcomes you desire for your business.

Here are some of the best ways to ensure you make the most of your business plan.

Consider your audience

When you write your business plan keep the language clear and simple, while considering the audience you are writing for.

This audience might include staff members, investors, financial institutions or potential buyers.

Keep these people in mind as you complete each section of the plan, factoring in exactly what they need to know.

Communicate it to your staff

Your business plan is the document that guides the future of your business, and your staff are your partners on this journey.

Do communicate your business plan with your staff.

This doesn't mean offering up the document in full, but instead ensuring they are aware of key sections including the operations plan, risk management, personnel plan and particularly your action plan.

Plan for growth

The key function of a business plan is to ensure your enterprise is viable into the future. Once your business has become established, that often involves assessing risks and planning for growth.

Your business plan should be used to outline these growth strategies, including resources required, actions that need to be taken and the financial implications.

Have it handy

Your business plan is not a document that should languish in a desk drawer or sit gathering dust on a shelf.

It is a living document that should be referred to and updated often.

Have your plan handy and refer to it when setting goals, implementing new strategies or when you are making business decisions.

Keep it updated

A business plan works best when you revisit it regularly and revise it accordingly. Then and only then is it a tool that can be set to work to chart continuous improvement and growth.

As a minimum, you should look at your business plan once a year. However, some highly successful businesses also work in 90-day or quarterly sprints where goals are clearly set out and achieved in line with their business plan.

Respond to change

As mentioned, a business plan is a living document, and it offers immense power when you use it to anticipate and respond to change.

This happens by identifying strengths, weakness, opportunities and threats and creating the action plan that you will implement to manage these.

It's important to note, even during the period when your business doesn't change, factors outside it might – whether that's the economic landscape, new competitors, supply issues or other elements that might be beyond your control.

When you identify these in your business plan, you are in a position to manage whatever comes your way.

Chapter 3 - Know your customer

Without them you wouldn't be in business, but how good are your strategies for finding, creating and caring for your customers?

We'd all like to think we rate A+ in how we attract and handle our clientele, but the truth is many businesses could do a bit better or could be missing a link in the vital chain.

So let's look at the basics of customer creation and care.

Do you know your customer?

"The purpose of business is to create and keep a customer." —
Peter F. Drucker

Every business has an ideal customer. This is the customer with the right mindset, right ethos and the right need for your services or goods.

You need to identify and know this person intimately – who they are, where they find information, and what drives them to make a purchasing decision. And this person may change throughout the life of a business.

Only when you know them, will you know how to find them, market to them and serve them well.

So take the time to consider who this person is, assign them a character profile, devise a qualifying statement and allow them a prime place in your business.

Put yourself in your customer's place

"The golden rule for every business man is this: Put yourself in your customer's place." – Orison Swett Marden

Know your customer and you'll know their habits, location, and the business image you need to portray. These are the essential ingredients that result in efficient marketing, creating a message that will be heard, and are also used to ensure your services meet a client's expectation.

When you know your customer and can put yourself in their place, you can envisage what they need to know about your business to have them walk through your doors.

Once there, you can further speak their language through the Vision and Mission of your business, the environment you provide, and the level and type of customer service that you offer.

Engage with your customer

"The more you engage with customers the clearer things become and the easier it is to determine what you should be doing." – John Russell

Customer care doesn't end at the point of sale. The best service is about establishing a long-term relationship that sees them return again and again. And to create this you need to have two-way communication.

This happens by seeking feedback from your clientele, asking them essential business questions like how they heard about you, how your product or service experience was for them, and how you as a business can improve.

It also involves actively listening to your customers during everyday interactions and working to rectify any reasonable gaps between their expectation and your service or product.

Meet your customer's expectations

"Your most unhappy customers are your greatest source of learning." – Bill Gates

You can have the best marketing, the flashest office and the most highly trained staff, but if there is a gap between what your customer expects and what you deliver then you need a course of action to resolve any issues.

While instances of discontent may be rare, it's critical every business has a customer complaints policy to deal with them. This policy not only provides your business with the tools to resolve foreseeable issues but outlines the chain of command and pinpoints who should become involved when something goes awry.

Importantly, a customer complaints policy prepares your business for handling any issues. It allows staff and management to envisage what the consumer expects and have additional means to meet that expectation even if it is not achieved in the first instance.

Key takeaway

Your customer is the reason you are in business, but even the best and most renowned corporations have been guilty of failing to understand their clientele or of losing sight of who they are.

You don't just need to know your customer when you start your business but understand them throughout the life of it; communicating with them, listening to them and meeting their changing needs. That's the core of business, and the key driver of whether it succeeds or fails.

Defining your ideal customer

You think you know your customer, right? They're the person who walks through your door, uses your services and happily comes back for more.

But how well do you really know this person that your business depends upon, and how do you find and appeal to others in their group?

The generally accepted way of defining your ideal customer is to ask many questions of available data to identify things such as; gender, age, education and income level, location, devices used, referral source, aspirations, fears, problems the product or service solves, path followed to find you - website or social media etc.

Answers to these questions help create an ideal customer profile.

Many claim that this form of identifying customers actually provides more than one description of an ideal customer. I guess that means that "the" ideal customer has not been identified! Perhaps this is not the best way of identifying your ideal customer.

An often used way of then managing customers identified using demographic information is to break them into four groups - A, B, C, & D.

Labelling the groups as A = Excellent; B = Okay; C = Not too bad; and D = Not Good, then allows for dispensing with all of the Ds and most of the Cs while trying to retain the As and most of the Bs.

It seems to me that if the outcome of obtaining customers in the generally accepted way is dispensing with some of those customers because they don't meet the description of Ideal Client, then the method is not delivering the desired outcome.

A better way of identifying your ideal client is to clearly identify what **solution** is provided and how that **impacts** a customer at a deep emotional level.

It is worth remembering that we make purchasing decisions emotionally. We justify them rationally and logically, but we make the decision emotionally.

You have only one ideal client.

There are many customers who will buy your product or service and then describe - at a surface level - the reason for purchasing in many and varied ways.

And each of your customers may appear in many different forms at a surface level.

However, if you look deep inside what is motivating the person to buy, you will find the emotional reason.

Having found that emotional reason, you can then identify the right words to attract that person and have them do business with you.

Customers discovered and obtained using this method typically bring all the attributes a business wants in a customer including:

- They value you
- They value what you do
- They value the way you do it
- They are more willing to pay
- They are ambassadors
- They bring less customer service issues
- and the list goes on.

When you know your ideal customer, marketing, advertising and sales is much easier because you 'know' what speaks directly to them. This makes your offer much more appealing since these customers already feel like your business understands their needs and wants.

After you 'know' who your ideal client really is, the demographic information - which applies to 'some' of your clients - becomes a valuable tool to assist with marketing.

These are the top tips for getting to know your customer and effectively reaching them...

Customer profiles

Every business should have a very clear idea of who their ideal customer is, and one way to define this is through a customer persona.

This fictional profile of who your target customer is and how they operate helps tailor your marketing, products and the services you provide.

Akin to having an imaginary friend in the room when making marketing or business decisions, a customer persona incorporates details of how your specific customer thinks, what they like to do, how much income they have at hand and where they like to go.

These are not vague details but very specific information about how this person operates and makes decisions.

A customer persona includes:

- How they spend most of an average day
- Their disposable income
- Brands they are attracted to
- Their position on a specific issue
- Their priorities in life

- Sources of information they trust
- Keywords that indicate who they are
- A quote which sums up their frame of thinking
- Goals they strive to meet

A customer persona is a fantastic method of finding information relevant to your ideal client and is therefore a tremendous help in your marketing.

However, a list of demographic information is not a description of your ideal client. If it was, every person who fits that description should be a customer of your business. And anyone who does not fit that description should not be a customer.

The description of your ideal client is something far deeper, far more specific and does not contain demographic information..

Market research

While creating a customer persona is an integral element to knowing who your ideal clientele are and how to market to them, it isn't the only element used to learn more about your market.

Further research involves discovering your market segment. A market segment differs from a customer persona in that it covers more general demographics like age, income, ethnicity and traits.

These are the statistics used to market to your customers, while the persona is the characterisation of your ideal client.

Marketing plans

Once you know your customer and the segment in which they operate you are best positioned to market directly to them. And this is where your marketing plan comes in.

A marketing plan should outline:

- How and where to advertise
- What mediums you should use
- The essential elements of your branding
- What vocabulary to use

Key takeaway: Learning more about your customer enables you to discover where they seek information, what calls them to action and the services that best suit their needs. It arms business with insightful information about who they're really targeting and enables you to hone your brand and message.

Creating a customer persona

A customer persona is not a brief description of the customer you'd like to have but instead a detailed biography of an individual that you have created from your target market with a name and image assigned to them.

This persona includes simple information like a name, age, education level, marital status and personality type.

It then goes on to take a deep dive into their goals, frustrations, decision making criteria, favoured brands and the channels they use to access information.

Researching your customer persona

There are numerous ways to compile the information you need to create a customer persona, but often it starts with the clients you already have.

After all, these are the people who have already bought from you so your business clearly resonates with them.

Take a good look at your current client database and analyse the shared traits these clients have, including their demographics.

Consider their shared attitudes and approach to life, along with the things that drive them to purchase your product or use your service.

Larger organisations will often also bring in their sales people to take part in this exercise, but it doesn't stop there.

Survey or interview

Surveying or interviewing your customers or prospects might sound like a daunting task but the results it yields can really help you hone your client persona.

Ideally, this involves a 10-15 minute phone chat and you can start it by asking whether they'd mind taking part in research that is aimed at serving them better.

You can also use the power of email surveys to complete this task.

If you're starting up and don't yet have customers, look at the reviews and testimonials of your competition to understand the common traits and attributes of your intended customer.

Online research

In the digital age, online research can be a hugely effective way of fleshing out your ideal customer's personality traits and motivators.

In many cases, you can really glean an insight into people via social media.

In the meantime the testimonials and reviews that previous customers have left you or your competition can offer a major insight into their pain points, frustrations and the type of service/ product they're looking for.

Assemble the information

Once you have your information at hand, it's time to assemble it and often you will be amalgamating a lot of research into simple paragraphs or sentences to describe who your customer persona is.

Once complete, you should create an avatar or use a picture to indicate who your ideal customer is. This gives you a better, more personable idea of exactly who you are talking to as a business, and the problems they need you to solve.

It changes over time

Finally, once your persona is complete, use it. Stick it on the wall in your office and run your marketing and business decisions by it.

What would your persona say to something, how would they respond to that type of marketing etc?

Also bear in mind this persona can change over time as your business expands, changes course and evolves – which is why a customer persona should be on your annual to-do list, along with updating your business plan.

Customer persona exercise

Demographic Method

Start with these questions:

1. What is the gender and age of these clients?

2. Where do they usually reside?

3. What is the educational background and general income range of the clientele?

4. To what does a typical consumer aspire? Who are their heroes?

5. What established sources are referring the customers to you?

6. How can our offer lend a hand in their routine?

7. What motivated them to select this option?

8. Was this an impulsive purchase or was there an urge generating it?

9. How much time elapsed between shopping and ultimately deciding to purchase?

10. How does the product alleviate the issue they face?

11. How soon will they begin making use of it?

12. Were there any additional related products procured with it?

13. What electronic devices are they using to browse the internet?

14. Prior to the purchase, have they interacted on your company website, social media or in real life, etc.?

15. What excites / frightens potential customers?

16. What do you do that they become excited about?

17. Do they respond to special marketing codes and / or discounts?

18. Was there subsequent engagement with other departments?

19. Have they referred others to you?

20. Are they opted in for newsletters etc.?

What is "really" motivating this customer method

Begin by asking yourself:

- ◆ What do I really want to do?
- ◆ How do I want to do it?
- ◆ When do I want to do it?
- ◆ Where do I want to do it?

- Who do I want to do it for?
- Why do I want to do it?
- Under what circumstances do I want to do it? (time / payment / conditions / etc.)

When you are satisfied that the answers are set - that is, they won't change because of someone else's opinion - move to the second part.

Now, with your ideal customer in mind, ask the following:

- How does that person want to interact with me?
- What is motivating that person to match what I do?
- How does that person want to hear of me / find me?

When you find the answers difficult to discover, ask history to help. The history of where we have been and how we have progressed to where we are now reveals the answers you need to identify how you and your business align with the view of your ideal client.

Understanding your ideal client at this level means you are in a position to eliminate most customer issues in your business. It allows you to do business in a simpler, more comfortable manner and enjoy the results that consequently flow with greater volume and ease.

In other words, you are able to more easily engage with more of your ideal clients more often.

The customer experience

"The Customer Experience". These three little words are critical to business success. Why? Because the customer experience is the key factor that determines whether a consumer will choose your business, stay with your business or recommend it to their peers.

So let's take a look at the customer experience including why it's something every business should consider every time they examine what's happening in their operation now and every time they ask what happens next.

The customer experience

Defined as "the product of an interaction between an organisation and a customer over the duration of their relationship", the customer experience encompasses every interaction a customer has with your brand.

It is marketing, customer service, and the quality of products you offer. It is the initial conversation on the phone, the interactions people have with your staff and the follow-up and satisfaction you provide.

The customer experience is often broken down into three key elements:

- the customer journey,
- the brand touchpoints the customer interacts with,
- the environments the customer experiences during their experience.

The customer journey

From the moment a potential client reaches your website, sees your ad, or hears about your business through others, the customer journey has begun.

This initial interaction sets the bar of what potential clients believe your business has to offer. Now it's down to you to ensure the promise equals their expectation at every touchpoint along the way.

Touchpoints

Every time a potential customer encounters your business it's a touchpoint, and these can live up to, fail to meet or exceed the experience a consumer expects.

As a business it's important to map out these touchpoints, breaking them down into a series of spheres.

Traditional touchpoints include:

Before purchasing

- Advertising
- Website
- PR
- Word of mouth
- Social media
- Promotions
- During purchase
- Reception
- Staff greeting/phone manner
- Premises location, look and feel (if applicable)
- Product range
- Price point

Post purchase

- Product quality
- Guarantees, warranties
- Follow-up
- Customer loyalty
- Service and support
- Billing
- Product installation or assistance
- Thank you cards

Experience

While it's critical to examine the touchpoints along your customer journey, the most important factor is to work out whether what you promise ties in with what you provide. And these are the questions to ask...

Pre-purchase

- Is your message relevant and relatable?
- Does your business website, marketing and advertising tell a consistent story?
- Does your message reflect your business in the best possible light?
- What do you say you offer?

During purchase

- Do you provide what you say you will?
- Are your staff aware of your promises? (As in your message, mission, vision and products)
- Are your staff trained to offer the best service? Do they know their role, your products and does their image correlate with your brand ethos?
- Have you given them the tools they need (process and procedures) to reflect your business in the best light?
- Is your service what you promise?
- Does your product meet the description?

Post purchase

- How do you gauge customer satisfaction?
- What is the resounding response of reviews or feedback?
- What is the ratio of repeat clientele?
- Do you know how you get customers? (Is it

recommendation, advertising, repeat clientele or all of the above?)

And the cycle continues. But only when the customer experience meets or exceeds their expectations will your business truly grow.

Seeking feedback

Customer feedback is critical throughout the business journey. While the numbers of business paint a picture as to what's going on, customer feedback and indeed staff feedback offers an insight into why.

But where and when should you seek feedback, and what will it allow you to learn?

Why feedback matters

Customer feedback provides a level of detail about your business that goes far beyond what your quarterly numbers and data may reveal.

In many ways it provides the 'why' of trends occurring within your business.

Importantly, customer feedback can reveal something is 'wrong', or 'right' long before that becomes apparent in your sales data and business ledgers.

This allows you to take action early, either doubling down on your efforts, or altering a product or service to better suit your ideal customer.

Meanwhile, seeking feedback from your clientele also helps foster a two-way conversation that indicates you value your customer's opinion and are prepared to alter your business or offering to meet their needs.

But how and where do you seek feedback?

Where to seek feedback

In reality, client feedback is all around us in business, but one of the best ways to understand how a customer is feeling or what they are experiencing is to ask.

So let's take a look at the different methods of gaining feedback.

Monitor social media

Comments on social media or ratings on Google provide an insight into how your customer felt about their experience with you or a product they have purchased.

These channels should be consistently monitored, and you should pay attention to the feedback provided.

Social media and reviews offer a critical insight into what your customers believe are the positives and negatives of dealing with your business.

Live chat

If your business has a live chat feature, it's worth analysing this to see if there are common questions, complaints or issues that arise.

Each of these can offer a clue into what's working and what may need improvement in terms of service or common questions and complaints your customers have about a product..

Phone enquiries

Like live chat, the phone enquiries your business receives provide an insight into common issues that your customers may be experiencing.

Consider, what type of themes emerge when it comes to phone calls made to your business? Do people need more information about how to use your product? Were they happy or unhappy with the level of service?

Customer feedback surveys

If you really want to get to the heart of how your customer feels, a simple customer feedback survey is a great option.

Whether you use an email survey, paper survey or draw on tools like dedicated survey software, a survey can really drill down into what your customer is experiencing when they deal with your business.

Net Promoter scores

Net promoter scores (NPS) provide an insight into how loyal your customer is likely to be to your brand.

Although not all businesses consistently monitor their NPS, it is a great way to see how your business is travelling and whether the customer experience is likely to see it primed for growth.

In short, ascertaining your NPS involves asking how likely someone is to recommend your product, services, business or brand to their network of peers.

The more people there are who are likely to recommend you, the better your business is performing.

Stay tuned, there's more on exactly how they work below.

Quarterly business reviews

Regular reviews of your business performance provide a big-picture perspective of how your operation is tracking. While these numbers can help identify when something is going awry, it's then about using the above tools to pinpoint the exact problem.

Compiling the data

With the feedback in hand, it's time to start distilling it so you can take action, and there are different ways to do this, depending on the size of your operation.

Some people opt for tools like Google sheets, where they input the information in categories, others draw on their CRM, or other automated analytical tools.

Regardless, the data needs to be compiled and analysed to find common themes and pain points throughout the customer journey that need to be remedied.

Acting on the feedback

Once you know what the issues are and where they're located in a business, it's time to create strategies, policies and procedures to fix any issues or bugs.

That means clearly defining the problem and allocating it to the right department to take the required action.

Closing the loop

The last stage of seeking feedback sees you 'close the loop'. This involves letting customers know you have heard them and have acted upon their feedback.

And again, there are a variety of ways to do this. You can thank customers for the feedback provided, reward them for their time, produce a report with the findings and strategies you have implemented, or let them know on your website/social media channels about your improved offering.

However, most importantly, the customer's next encounter with your brand should reflect the changes you have made in a bid to improve their experience.

After all, actions speak far louder than words, and nothing indicates how valuable a customer is to you than listening to them and tailoring the experience to their liking.

What is a Net Promoter Score?

Net promoter scores are a great way of ascertaining how a business is performing courtesy of their ability to determine how loyal a customer is to a brand.

So let's recap what they are and how they work.

First developed in about 2003, Net Promoter Scores are a simple way of gauging customer loyalty to a brand.

To begin to understand your net promoter score, the first question is:

'On a scale of 0-10, how likely is it you would recommend our company/product/service to a friend?'

- Those who respond 9 and 10 are considered **Promoters**, in that they are likely to be true advocates for your brand and exhibit value-adding behaviours like purchasing further products, or making positive referrals to other potential customers.
- Those returning a score of 7 or 8 are considered **Passives**.
- Those returning 0 to 6 are **Detractors**, meaning they are less likely to exhibit value-adding behaviour, and may actually work against your business.

In other words:

- **Promoters** (score 9-10) are loyal advocates who will keep buying and refer others, facilitating business growth.
- **Passives** (score 7-8) are satisfied but not passionate customers. They may be vulnerable to competitive offerings.
- **Detractors** (score 0-6) are unhappy customers who can damage your brand and impede growth through negative word-of-mouth.

Calculating the NPS

The net promoter score is an integer derived by subtracting the percentage of respondents who are Detractors from the percentage of respondents who are Promoters. Passives are simply included in the number of overall respondents.

Or: (Number of Promoters — Number of Detractors) / (Number of Respondents) x 100

An example

Say for example you survey 1000 respondents, with 650 falling into the Promoter category, 100 considered Passives, and 250 Detractors.

The equation would then equal: (650-250)/1000 x 100, which equals a net promoter score of 40.

Ultimately, the NPS can range from a low of -100 (if every customer is a Detractor) to a high of +100 (if every customer is a Promoter).

However, statistics indicate the average response is +32 while the lower quartile of performers are below zero and the upper quartile are above 70.

Not an isolated question

Although the beauty of the NPS is in the simplicity of the initial question, it doesn't work in isolation.

As part of customer feedback, businesses will first ask 'how likely is it that you would recommend our company/product/service to a friend?' and then go on to identify areas for improvement along with why clients have given a business that score.

So, for example a simple customer survey will include the following questions.

- On a 0-to-10 scale, how likely is it that you would

recommend us (or this product or service) to a friend or colleague?

- What is the primary reason for your score?
- Why?
- What could we do better?

Together, this information enables a business to identify how happy clients currently are with their services and the areas where they could improve.

Why Net Promoter Scores matter

As a simple figure, Net Promoter Scores allow a business to quickly and effectively gauge exactly how a client feels about their products and services, and many Fortune 1000 enterprise managers note it's the first figure they check each and every day.

Understanding your Net Promoter Score gives you an insight into whether your business is providing the customer experience you hope it does.

Meanwhile, drilling into the why behind the score enables a business to take action when products or services fail to hit the mark.

Importantly Net Promoter Scores capture consumer sentiment before it becomes negative word of mouth or a complete image crisis.

The positive in the negative – handling feedback

We'd all like to imagine every review left by a customer would speak of our business and its products or services in glowing terms. Sometimes, that simply isn't the case and that negative feedback can have you reeling.

But even in the negatives there are positives to be found. It's a matter of understanding the message and working out whether and how it will improve your business overall.

Here's a guide to finding the positive in the negative when it comes to poor reviews.

"Your most unhappy customers are your greatest source of learning." - Bill Gates

In business all feedback is valuable but it's how you interpret and use it that counts. Most importantly, this feedback should be considered a useful tool for better serving your ideal customer.

So how do you assess and utilise a negative comment or review?

It comes down to the who, the why, the what and then the how.

The who, the why, the what, the how

When handling negative feedback consider the following:

Who is your feedback coming from?

It's a plain and simple truth that you cannot keep all people happy all the time.

When you receive negative feedback it's very important to ascertain whether the feedback is coming from your ideal customer, a person you are attempting to bring in as a customer, or perhaps someone who is otherwise unattached to your business.

In business, the person you are trying to please is your ideal customer. If a person is not your ideal customer, chances are they will find a negative in your products or offerings because your business is not relevant to them.

In other words, your business is not targeted to or looking to cater to their needs, so the negative may matter less.

Why are you receiving this feedback?

As with anything, it's important to view feedback in context.

What is the motivation of the complainant? Did they use your product and service as intended, did they have an unpleasant experience with your business or are they simply having a bad day?

What is the message in the feedback?

That said, in most things there is a grain of truth. So, take the time to look at the feedback and get to the root of the message involved.

Is there an element of truth in their feedback that you need to consider to better serve your ideal customer?

How will you respond?

If the comments are coming from your ideal customer and there is truth or an important message in what they are saying, the next step is to consider how you will respond.

How will you address the issue with them as an individual? What will you offer to rectify the situation or reasonably satisfy them?

More importantly, what will you change about your product, procedures or systems to improve your business in the future.

As British Airways Vice President Donald Porter once famously said: "Customers don't expect you to be perfect. They do expect you to fix things when they go wrong".

It's how you use it that matters

Feedback can be incredibly valuable in business, offering you an outside perspective of how your business can improve, grow and better cater to its customer.

But as with all things, it's how you interpret, understand and utilise that feedback, regardless of whether it is positive or negative that counts.

10 tools for seeking feedback

- Email surveys using software such as Survey Monkey
- Hard copy survey questions, distributed by your business in-person or via post
- Survey kiosks, comprising a mobile tablet and software positioned at your business
- Phone surveys of existing clientele
- Social media monitoring
- Google ratings and reviews
- Reviews and testimonials
- In-person feedback
- Common customer questions or complaints
- Customer focus groups

Chapter 4 - Vision and Mission

In business, we hear a lot about Visions and Missions – these bold statements etched into the websites and walls of businesses and big corporations.

But amidst all the careful crafting, big hopes and dreams, why are these words so important, what's the difference between a Vision and a Mission, and where do you begin when it comes to creating them?

Here's why Vision and Mission Statements are more than just words.

The difference between Vision and Mission

Alike in the way they are created, the Vision and Mission Statements factor in two separate stages of your business and are used in different ways.

The Vision is about where you want to go, encapsulating your broader business goals, reflecting your view of the world and your ultimate place within it. It calls your team to a sense of greater purpose, looking to the future of what you could achieve.

Meanwhile, the Mission talks about your current position, what you are doing now, and how you do it. It's used to let your customers know what you offer and that they're in the right place, while guiding your employees in the way they do business.

Both can be as short as a single sentence but should be carefully thought through to encompass your goals and operation. A great example of the difference and application is Google.

Google's Vision: "To provide access to the world's information in one click".

Google's Mission: "To organise the world's information and make it universally accessible and useful".

While their Vision Statement is grand, futuristic, all-encompassing and ambitious, their Mission Statement speaks to the now and their day-to-day role, organising information in a useful and accessible manner.

The Mission is the immediate methodology behind how they will meet their Vision.

Creating a Vision Statement

The Vision Statement defines the core ideals of a business and gives it ambitious direction.

A Vision Statement does not need to describe what you do, but rather the end point – where you want to go or the resultant experience or outcome. Based on your business goals, it should not be overly complicated and it should be easy to recall.

It will answer the question: "where are we going?" Not "how will we get there?". And the best way to create a Vision Statement is to draw from your most important business goals.

Your Vision Statement should be:

- Succinct
- Simple (in plain English)
- Short (saying a lot in a few words)
- Passionate
- Memorable
- Powerful
- Realistic
- Outcome focussed (describing the ideal state for your business)
- Inspirational (building a picture of who you are in people's minds)

How to create your Vision

A Vision is a vivid mental image of what you want your business to be at some point in the future, based on your goals and aspirations. Having a Vision will give your business a clear focus, and can stop you heading in the wrong direction.

The best way to formalise and communicate the Vision you have for your business is to write a Vision Statement.

A Vision Statement captures, in writing, the essence of where you want to take your business, and can inspire you and your staff to reach your goals.

What to include in a Vision Statement

A Vision Statement should communicate your long-term business goals, and it should reflect your view of the world and your business' place in it.

It should also answer the fundamental question, 'Where are we going?'. The practical aspect of 'How will we get there?' is usually dealt with in a Mission Statement or a business plan.

Your Vision Statement might be inspired by certain aspects of your business, such as:

- finances (i.e. to sustain and support your family)
- reputation (i.e. amongst customers, staff, competitors)
- service quality standards (i.e. to make customers a priority)
- growth (i.e. you offer new products, innovate, get more customers, increase locations)
- passion (i.e. that you and your staff enjoy what you do)
- sustainability (i.e. that you are financially and environmentally sustainable).

You should also think about what inspired you to start a business, and what business values and principles are important to you.

How to write a Vision Statement

To write an effective Vision Statement you should think about what your business does, and imagine what your business would look like if it became the best possible version of itself.

Hold a business Vision workshop

A good first step in developing a Vision Statement is to invite your key staff to a business vision workshop.

By brainstorming and sharing ideas, you can answer fundamental questions about the direction of your business, which will make it much easier to write your Vision Statement.

Writing a Vision Statement

After you've held your vision workshop and come up with some ideas, it's time to write your official Vision Statement. Make sure your Vision Statement:

- is clear and written in plain English (i.e. no jargon or 'business speak')

- is passionate, powerful and memorable
- is short and says a lot in a few words
- is realistic (i.e. in terms of your resources, capabilities and growth potential)
- describes the best outcome (ideal state) for your business
- doesn't use numeric measures of success
- helps build a picture in people's minds.

Example Vision Statements

Large companies often have a grand Vision Statement that aspires to global goals. But even a small business can benefit from having a relatively grand Vision Statement. Below are some examples of Vision Statements from global companies, as well as small businesses with local goals:

- 'There will be a personal computer on every desk running Microsoft software.' (Microsoft's original Vision Statement)
- 'Our vision is to be earth's most customer centric company; to build a place where people can come to find and discover anything they might want to buy online.' (Amazon.com)
- 'To build a community of coffee lovers in Brisbane, by serving the best coffee at the best possible prices.' (local café)
- 'Our salon will change the way you think about a haircut, and leave you glowing both inside and out.' (local hairdresser)

Using your Vision Statement

A Vision Statement isn't something you write and then forget.

As your business grows, you should constantly revisit your Vision

Statement to measure your progress and success. It can also help you make key business decisions, because it represents the heart and soul of your business.

Many businesses use their Vision to help create a unique selling proposition, which is the marketing statement you use to sell your products and services.

It's a good idea to make your business' Vision Statement visible in the workplace to inspire your staff and remind them of their purpose, for example, by:

- posting it in staff common areas
- including it in any code of conduct documents
- using it as a tool in staff performance reviews

You can also promote your business' Vision Statement publicly by displaying it in your business or using it in marketing material.

Your Mission Statement

As mentioned earlier, your Mission Statement serves a very different purpose to that of your Vision.

The Mission talks about your current position, what you are doing now, who your ideal customer is and how you meet their needs.

This makes it slightly more complicated to create than your overarching Vision, but when you get it right, it is key to the way your business operates.

Creating your Mission Statement

The Mission Statement delivers several key pieces of information about your business operation now.

It outlines:

- What the needs or opportunities are that the business addresses

- What the business of the organisation is
- How customer needs are addressed
- What level of service is provided
- What values guide the organisation

Your Mission Statement is also the beginning of every answer to any question you are ever likely to be asked about your business by any person regardless of their relationship to the business.

The Mission Statement should deliver its message clearly to everyone who comes in contact with your business – customers, employees, suppliers and other stakeholders.

It will inspire, support and encourage engagement, giving a clear view of outcomes.

A good Mission Statement does all of the above and clearly shows a new customer they are 'in the right place'. It is drawn from your ethos and operations.

Ideally, the Mission Statement should identify your ideal client; explain how you serve them (*solve their problem*) and give them comfort that they are the most important part of your business.

When created well, the **Mission Statement** contains within it the **Qualifying Statement** (a statement which allows your [potential] client to identify themselves to you).

Creating the Mission Statement

What the Mission Statement should deliver:

- What is/are the objective/s of the entity
- What the entity does (physical)
- What the entity delivers
- What the customer gets (outcome/s)

Tip: Consider words commonly used by the client. Make it non-discriminatory, including the client's wants, and the emotional benefits/outcomes to the client.

Parts that make up a good Mission Statement

- Establish how the entity is to be perceived. Stake a claim to this position.

- What's in it for me? (reader/listener)

- Who do you want to be part of the entity; who will nominate themselves as a potential client – or disqualify themselves.

- What the entity 'does'

- What the entity delivers (for the individual customer)

- How the entity feels about its client/customer

- How the entity reacts to/interacts with its client/customer

- The entity is about business, but there is fun and friendship

- Reiterating the primary purpose

- How the entity tells others – and what it tells

- Another way we are known/found

- Reminding the client/customer it is a commitment (in the nicest possible way)

- Referencing the business' growth

- It's not just about the entity's relationship with the client, but also has a relationship with the wider community

- Always focused on 'Doing the right thing'

- Recognising the need for a strong commercial base

- Reiterating the business is about giving not taking

Paragraphs that make up a good Mission Statement

- What you do - Not what you 'do' physically, but what outcome/s you achieve on behalf of clients.

- This references the answer to the question generated by para 1 but then goes a step further to reveal how you do that.
- Information supporting Para 2.
- Further supporting information – Giving comfort that what is stated in Para 1 really is attainable.
- What you get out of it – Why you do what you do.

The Mission Statement helps a person identify, in seconds, whether they want to be part of your journey.

It provides answers to the questions confronting a potential new customer.

When written well, the Mission Statement can be delivered with great effect either verbally or in writing and gives a person comfort that they are in the right place or alternatively clearly shows they are not.

Either way, as a business owner, that is a good result.

Communicating your Vision and Mission

Creating your Vision and Mission are only the first stage of the journey. Then these statements need to be communicated to your staff, clients and stakeholders.

Write them large

Your Vision and Mission should be displayed prominently within your business and also beyond it, in things like your logos, and official correspondence.

Educate your staff

Your staff should be educated about your Vision and Mission, including how this translates to your business values.

Not only should they be aware of the Vision and Mission, but they should also know them and be encouraged to draw on them when making decisions in your business.

Use in your marketing

Both your Vision and Mission form the basis of all advertising. Although they may not be incorporated in your marketing verbatim, their message or ethos will be conveyed in every marketing material your business issues.

Refer to them when making business decisions

Finally, every decision you make about your business should be considered through the lens of your business Vision and Mission - from the staff you hire to products you sell, and the clients you take on.

Why Visions and Missions matter

Vision and Mission Statements may be just words, but they are part of the future and current definition of your business.

Together, they keep a business and its staff on track as a constant reminder of achievement now and into the future.

Like most areas of your business, they will need to be revisited and revised as your business evolves.

The Vision Statement creates inspiration in all who hear it.

For staff, this can be the reason they come in - to be part of the journey delivering something of value to their community.

For a potential client/customer it gives a reason for that person to also be part of the exciting journey.

For the business owner, this Vision reminds you of the business goals (ultimate and intermediate) and again becomes the reason for 'getting up' and coming into the office.

Chapter 5 - Sales

Quite simply, selling is the art of getting to know someone and solving a problem better than anyone else.

Every business is based on selling. Whether it's services, skills or products, the fundamental principle of enterprise is providing something a customer needs, presenting it to them as a viable option and providing it in a professional manner.

So why is 'selling' one of the most challenging components of business?

Well let's look at selling in a different light...

Selling without fear

Every business needs to 'Sell' but 'Sales' is a word and concept that often scares business owners and customers.

The idea of 'putting yourself out there' to promote a service or product can feel beyond the comfort zone while the term 'sales' can conjure negative connotations of high-energy, hard-pedalling techniques that do not necessarily reflect how true selling really works.

The truth is, sales doesn't have to be scary. It is actually a very natural part of business, involving everyday conversations with people who have a genuine interest in what you have to offer.

The art of it comes down to finding the right people to speak with, knowing why your product or service will genuinely assist them, and offering it in a way that comes naturally to all involved.

Selling is problem solving

Since the first trader set up a stall to provide wares in exchange for currency, selling has been about solving a problem – food to eat, clothes to wear, expertise to utilise.

The world has thrived on it, building empires on the sale and trade of sugar, spices, cotton or coffee.

And it's no different in this day and age. Selling is about identifying what people need and providing it to them. Modern business may be more about technology and lifestyle, but the problem solving required is essentially the same.

Selling is a conversation

Given that business revolves around selling and selling is getting to know someone and solving a problem better than anyone else, it is worth recognising that this is nothing more than a conversation.

Anyone can have a conversation.

The conversation required to deliver best outcomes is remarkably simple, however it does require some skill.

When it comes to having a conversation that results in a sale, you must first understand two critical things:

- what do you actually deliver?
- who will benefit from that product/service?

And it's important to remember, should you discover that a prospect (as in someone with whom you are having a conversation about solving a problem) is not someone you can help, this is as good an outcome as discovering that you can assist them.

Discovering you can help them then introduces the need for further skill.

At this point it's about delivering the information required to have the prospect 'see' the result as their solution, rather than delivering the information in a way that creates uncertainty in the mind of the prospect and therefore no desire to work with you.

Selling is about clarity

One of the fundamental factors that many business owners overlook, is that selling is simply about clarity.

It is about creating clarity as to who your ideal customer is (the person you should be talking with).

It involves clarity about what you offer, and why it benefits your ideal customer.

It further requires clarity about how you provide that product or service in a way that is different, or better, than anyone else.

Having this clarity of understanding removes any sense of overwhelm and chaos.

And that has benefits for both you and your customer. When you create clarity you are on the path to certainty.

And certainty is success..

The sales process

Each of us sells in everything we do. Leaders sell a vision, parents sell values, and salespeople sell products or services.

Breaking down the wall

Sales often takes a similar form. A business identifies a potential customer who might begin to put up a wall.

This wall is built on excuses, reasons and objections, and it's the prospect's way of saying 'I don't want what you've got', or 'you haven't given me sufficient reason to want what you have'.

Often this wall goes up as soon as someone spots a salesperson. The prospect may not even know at that point what the salesperson is offering.

The salesperson's job then becomes knocking down that wall, one objection at a time. Theoretically once each objection has been removed, the prospect is brought to the 'right decision' where they buy the services or products on offer.

To prepare to sell, you need to first build your story.

You need to know your product or service, you also need to know your processes and procedures for delivering that product or service.

In other words, you need to know the customer journey from start to finish - from the why behind a business' origin to the experience a customer has using the products or services, and also why a customer may no longer use your products or services.

This creates clarity on what it is you are actually selling, it helps determine who the customer is who will want that product or service, and then determine whether the ideal customer you are speaking with actually does want that product or service at that moment in time.

When a customer is brought into a business, they become a stakeholder, and need a track to run on - a track which is simple for them to follow.

Build rapport and gain trust

Regardless of what you are selling, first you must build rapport and gain trust.

When you meet someone, you need to meet them well – be present, don't take them for granted, ensure they are in a position to give you appropriate attention at a suitable time.

Then it's about asking the right questions and listening to their answers.

These questions should relate directly to what the prospect wants to achieve. If it cannot be achieved with what you have, it's time to step away.

In asking those questions, it shows your prospect you are present and interested in their outcomes.

Concentrate on the prospect, not you. It's about achieving their outcomes, and then more often than not, they will decide they trust you.

Bringing the prospect to the right decision

You might assume the right decision is that the customer buys the product or service you have on offer.

As far as I'm concerned that's absolutely not the case. In order for a successful sale to eventuate, three things need to occur:

- The prospect must <u>need</u> the item on offer
- The prospect must be <u>capable of paying</u> for that product or service
- The prospect must <u>want to pay</u> for that product or service

When we talk about bringing the customer to the right decision, it doesn't mean that they will or should buy your product on every occasion.

If the product is not the right fit for them, there is no point selling to them. It will only lead to a dissatisfied customer and potentially create customer service issues in the future.

Find facts, identify the problem and the wish

When you are talking to a prospect, you should be asking all sorts of questions about what it is that they do that is relevant to your product or service.

You are looking for the criteria they would use in order to decide that your product or service is actually going to deliver what they want.

Through appropriate questioning, you will find the facts and criteria that they will rely on to make the decision that will solve the problem that they have and deliver the wish that they seek.

This might involve a long conversation because they need to build their trust in you in order to deliver the right answers.

Time with a prospect can be well spent or poorly spent

Beginning without a well-furnished and properly constructed presentation is inviting loss of direction, lack of clarity, failure, and disappointment.

If you are not presenting what your ideal client wants, they will not do business with you.

If you understand who you want as your ideal client, what it is that client wants to purchase, and you are actually providing that product of service, you have already won, they might just need a little help to understand it.

Statement of Intent

Your Statement of Intent is what will allow you to move from being a visitor to being the one in charge of what is transpiring. This is where you politely but emphatically put your prospect at ease while you explain how events will unfold from this point on. This 'Statement' should identify:

1. Why you are there – To discover if you can assist with / provide a solution to / help you achieve some of your... It is the need that your product addresses.

2. How you will achieve this – To do this I will ask you some questions about...

3. Who you are – Explain who XYZ business is and what you do.

4. What you will do – Thirdly examine how ... (the product / service / business) can help the client achieve their ... goals.

Then the dialogue might go as follows:

"Now, if I could improve one thing about your ... situation, what would give you the most benefit?

Answer: ...

At this point you know what key item must be addressed to allow a sale to occur.

Make the presentation

Your presentation should be skilfully put together in order to address the precise criteria the prospect has indicated they need.

In other words, it covers all of the facts that the prospect has mentioned that they'll need to understand in order to make a decision.

As you go through the conversation, whenever you come to a key point, ask for confirmation from the prospect that this is satisfying the need that they expressed earlier.

As you cover off all the needs that they have expressed, that means that your close is exceptionally simple.

The close

The close, done properly, is actually the easiest part of the sale. It's about asking for the sale.

If you have engaged in an authentic conversation with your prospect, by the time you get to the close, they know that everything that they wanted addressed has been covered.

Along the way they have also agreed with you that everything they wanted covered has been.

Asking someone to buy something formally is a very simple process. It could be "so when would you like it delivered?" or "when should we start?"

The 10 major ingredients to a sale

Sales is not a matter of luck; nor is it simply a numbers game.

There is some truth in the suggestion, "If you talk to enough people you will make (enough) sales".

The clever salesperson, however, studies his/her craft and, like any other professional, plies that craft with great skill to ensure the achievement of clearly established goals.

Just as there are methods and order to follow when baking a cake to achieve the best result, there are methods to follow when undertaking sales.

The system is this:

1. Break the prospect's preoccupation
2. Introduce yourself – (Yourself and the company/business)
3. Relax the prospect – (Talk about the prospect)
4. Introduce the product – (Peak curiosity – statement of intent)
5. Gather the details for the sale
6. Sell (create) the need – (make the best presentation ever!)
7. Ask for the sale
8. Rebut refusal (excuses)
9. Close the deal – (get the 'Yes!' and complete the paperwork)
10. Get the money – (There is no sale until it's paid for!)

Chapter 6 - Processes & procedures

Processes and procedures are the fine print of business. They are the nuts and bolts of how we go about business and are an often-underrated ingredient of business success.

There are three key reasons process and procedure matter and why no business should be without them.

Clear communication

Outlining your process and procedure is about informing your staff what you expect will happen, how it will occur, and who will be responsible for the task.

It allows you and your staff to do their job effectively and is, at its heart, the recipe for how your business works.

Good process and procedure means fewer employees – not necessarily a smaller staff base – but fewer employees to achieve a given or greater result. It allows your staff to also meet their goals, knowing what is expected of them.

In short, process and procedure is about:

- Writing everything down
- Leaving nothing to chance
- Everything working to a plan

Easy evaluation

Once you have given your business clear process and procedure, you have given it the opportunity to be evaluated. You can quickly discover what works, what doesn't and what areas need to be improved.

It allows you to see if there are gaps in the way you handle your sales, your service and your overall operation, and it gives you a means to correct any faults.

Your process and procedure should be an evolving document tailored to suit your business as it grows.

Clarity

Process and procedure is also about bringing your own clarity to the big picture of your business. It's about dispensing with the vague and clearly identifying what needs to occur on a day-to-day basis in order to achieve your big-picture goals.

It's the nitty-gritty of your operation that eliminates ambiguity and allows you to deal with everything from customer complaints to staff absences in a controlled and effective manner.

Processes and procedures are a small part of the greater workings of business, but one that should be part of your plan for success.

It's a step on the path to how you achieve your goals, and it's one that assists your staff, your customers and your business.

How to implement processes and procedures

Before we dive into how to implement processes and procedures, let's first take a look at the definition of each along with how they differ from standards or policies.

Processes and procedures are how things are done. They include all logical steps that need to be taken to achieve the desired result.

Meanwhile, a standard or policy is the expected behaviour that accompanies the completion of any task.

For example, a retailer might implement:

- a **process** to achieve sales
- create mandatory **procedures** for staff that are opening and closing the business daily
- set a **standard** (policy) for staff clothing and quality of customer service

Why they matter

Processes and procedures are all about consistency. Drawing on what is proven to work, they eliminate discrepancies within the operation and remove the variable that might impact the result.

Processes and procedures are particularly important when you start a business, but are equally valuable when a business is underperforming or you wish to improve the bottom line.

They then assist with the training of staff, and set a level of expectation within any enterprise.

What processes and procedures do

- Increase efficiency
- Provide consistency
- Allow for repeatable and scalable success

- Reduce the time a business owner spends supervising staff

What standards and policies do

- Set benchmarks staff must meet
- Define service levels
- Improve the customer experience
- Increase the likelihood of repeat clientele

When to implement processes and procedures

Processes and procedures should be implemented in all areas of a business that require consistency - whether that's the way a product is made and quality checked, how your business opens and closes each day, or how your business manages complaints.

Processes and procedures are also applied to areas like Workplace Health & Safety, and staff training.

In many ways these processes and procedures become a standardised checklist of what needs to occur at a set time in order for your business to perform at its best.

When to implement standards and policies

Standards set a level of expectation that your staff, products and overall business is expected to meet.

Standards apply to things like customer service, behaviour, workplace attire or uniforms, or the quality of the products that you manufacture.

Prime areas where policies, procedures or standards might be implemented include:

- Customer service (how to greet the customer, language used, when to make contact, preferred method of contact etc)

- Sales practices including scripts and policies such as guarantees, warranties and refunds.
- Marketing and promotion including preferred channels, preferred tone, branding style guides.
- Staff training, such as an onboarding procedure for all new staff and extending to performance reviews.
- Environmental practices within your business such as waste management policies and recycling.
- Management responsibilities.
- Workplace Health & Safety policies.
- Manufacturing procedures for the creation of products.
- Record keeping procedures and money management within the business.
- Use of technology including the rules around staff usage.

How to create processes, procedures and standards for your business

Like your business plan, your policies, procedures and standards are all living documents that change and evolve over the life of your business.

So let's look at how they are defined and implemented.

1. Identify a need

Policies, procedures and standards are designed to ensure best-practice within your business.

Their genesis lies in defining a need for something to be standardised in order for the activity to be performed more efficiently, more safely or to achieve a consistent outcome.

They might also be created in anticipation of a need. For example, if your business is set to manufacture a new or different product, procedures for its manufacture will be required.

Every business should be constantly reassessing its operating environment to see whether new policies, procedures or standards are required.

2. Consult with staff

As the people on the frontline of your business, your staff are often best placed to tell you what should be included in a process or procedure in order for an activity to be consistently performed well.

When developing policies and procedures, consult with staff about how they envisage it will work.

3. Delegate responsibility

Someone within your business should assume responsibility for drafting the process or procedure.

That might be you as the business owner, or it could be a member of your staff with expertise in that specific area.

4. Gather information

Are there external factors you need to account for within your policies, processes or procedures.

For example some policies will be guided by legal requirements or Workplace Health & Safety considerations.

Take the time to gather information that will help inform best practice.

5. Draft the policy and consult

A suitable process or procedure might require a few drafts. Once a draft has been put together, have it reviewed by the staff affected in order to gain feedback about its viability.

6. Finalise

Once a process or procedure meets the standards you hoped for, finalise it by making it available to staff and educating them about it.

Your policies, procedures and standards should be readily available to all staff within the business.

New staff should also be made aware of all relevant policies and procedures during onboarding.

7. Revise and hone

Policies, procedures and standards change as a business does. They are also impacted by external factors like law or technology.

Regularly revisit your policies and procedures to ensure they remain relevant and honed when required.

Ensuring your processes and procedures are effective

For processes and procedures to be effective in your business, they should be:

Documented

All policies and procedures should be in written form and made available to staff.

A standard operating procedures manual is a good way to house all your policies and procedures in one place.

Part of staff training

All new staff should be trained about the policies and procedures applicable to their role.

Regular general staff training should also be conducted to ensure staff remain aware of a business' policies and procedures.

Reflect the business Vision

Policies and procedures do not operate in isolation, they should reflect the Vision and strategy of your business.

Be general and specific

There are two layers to the standards and policies that govern your business: general policies and procedures, and then role or task specific procedures.

Practised by management

For your policies and procedures to be truly effective, they should be seen to be practised by the leaders within your business.

Staff are more likely to adhere to set guidelines if they see managers practising what they preach.

Discussed

Policies and procedures within a business should be openly discussed - whether that's in meetings or one-on-one with staff members.

This allows for feedback and improvement.

Open to improvement

On that note, policies and procedures should be open to improvement. Staff should feel they are stakeholders in their creation and evolution.

The policies and procedures can then be honed and improved over time.

Designed to empower

Policies and procedures should be created with a view to empowering your staff, not constraining them with rigid rules.

They allow your staff to take the appropriate action at the right time in the interests of successful outcomes.

Reviewed and updated

As I've mentioned, policies and procedures should be regularly reviewed and updated. This is especially the case if these guidelines are grounded in law.

Chapter 7 - The numbers of business

In business we talk a lot about numbers. We just love those 'numbery' terms - 'break even', 'profit and loss', 'sales conversion', and the list goes on.

So why the numerical obsession? Because at the end of the day numbers are the difference between failure and success.

Your numbers, including break-even analysis, future projections, and profit and loss, are also a large element of your business plan that reveals where you are now, what you need to earn, and where you would like to be.

To maintain forward motion, it's critical your numbers are current and accurately reflect the state of your business now as well as its projections for the future.

But there's more to numbers than take-home sales, and profit and loss.

The great thing about numbers is, unlike people, reports or plans,
NUMBERS NEVER LIE.

They are a trusted ally who will stare you straight in the face and reveal one single thing—THE TRUTH.

This makes numbers a valuable tool that can always be put to good use in business. Numbers not only reveal the ultimate outcome, they allow you to measure the little actions that contribute to the big picture of business.

Numbers give you the power to ascertain exactly what's working within a business, and what needs improvement. They identify the leaks, highlight areas of weakness, and reveal the right points to direct your attention.

Critically, they then allow you to analyse the action required to change the numbers of the future. It's all about measuring and adjusting, so here's what you need to know...

What you need to measure

"If you cannot measure it you cannot manage it."

Considering where to look for the numbers is simple:

In business we measure any point of the process where something can go wrong.

That's any point of the manufacturing, sales or delivery chain where a variation may occur, a leak can happen or a system may fail.

Say part of your business relies on salespeople, who you're paying to do a job. You need to know how effective your team is as a whole, how good an individual is at their role and how well the script is assisting them in their task.

Let's look at the numbers...

In this case we'd measure the following:

1. How many contacts each salesperson has been allocated

2. How many times an individual salesperson has contacted their lead

3. How many times they attempted to tell their story (make the presentation)

4. Whether they managed to complete their sales script (if not, how far through did they get?)

5. How many times they asked their contact to buy

6. How many sales they ultimately made

So, now we've got some lovely numbers, but what do they mean? Well the numbers for the above will tell you all sorts of things.

Part one might reveal the following:

- The contacts each salesperson receives are few and far between.
  The problem: Probably your marketing, possibly your appointment setter.

- Each salesperson receives lots of contacts but some do better than others at making it through their pitch.
  The problem: Possibly your sales script, but probably your salesperson, as some are having success.

- Each salesperson receives lots of contacts but few make it through their pitch.
  The problem: Definitely your sales pitch, possibly all your salespeople, and the person who hires them as well.

And that's just question one. As we extrapolate the findings we learn all sorts of things about the workings of our business. But the task doesn't end there because now we have the opportunity to adjust.

What the numbers tell us

"It is much more difficult to measure non-performance than performance" - Harold S. Geneen

Armed with a wealth of numbers we have the insight to analyse the critical workings of business, allowing us the opportunity to adjust.

In the case above we may find our sales pitch needs revision, our salesperson needs a confidence boost, or the training needs to be honed.

We may also discover a wealth of other interesting facts: like the appointment setter lacks confidence in a very specific salesperson, therefore they're allocating a series of dud leads.

Now we know the numbers and exactly what's occurring, we can take action to ensure the result that the business requires, asking a very simple question:

How do we change the action to get the outcome we want?

And this is a critical step in the measuring and adjusting chain. Numbers are useless if you fail to change the result.

Put simply, the numbers:

- ◆ Don't lie
- ◆ Reveal what's occurring in your business
- ◆ Illustrate what needs to change
- ◆ Provide the basis of how you need to change

Now it's down to you to adjust and alter the result...

Know your numbers task

What are the key elements of your business where a variation can occur?

What are the five questions you can ask to measure these areas?

List the results, what have you found?

What do these numbers show?

What areas do you need to change?

How do you intend to change them and adjust?

Past performance may "speak a tremendous amount about one's ability and likelihood for success", but in the words of Confucius:

"When it is obvious that the goals cannot be reached, don't adjust the goals, adjust the action steps."

Key Performance Indicators

Understanding where you're at and where you're off to in business involves pulling back the veil on the workings of your operation.

It means looking at each element where variations can occur to find what's successful, what's predictable and what can be improved.

Every business owner should be regularly looking at very specific elements of their operation to see what's occurring, and to do this we need to establish those all-important key performance indicators (KPIs).

The likelihood is key performance indicators will vary from one business to the next, but all operations will share at least a few common KPIs.

In a nutshell, KPIs should be applied to any area of your business where something can go "other than right". I call them [K]Critical Points of Interaction.

From there you can drill down deeper to gain a very comprehensive snapshot of how your business is operating now, could operate and will likely operate within the coming months.

So let's take a look at KPIs and what you should be measuring.

Critical KPIs

While operations vary from industry to industry and business to business, there are three common areas that all will share when it comes to measuring KPIs.

These are:

- Sales (revenue)
- Production (delivery)
- Cashflow (outgoings against income)

Now let's break it down.

Measuring sales

Let's be blunt. Every business is based on sales, whether you're a shopfront, service provider or online store.

Measuring your sales involves investigating the critical points of how you achieve them within your industry, so there are a series of points to look at including:

1. The number of contacts made

In simple terms this is how many people your business contacts, where there is the potential to make a sale.

In a bricks and mortar store this is simple traffic counting. In a traditional sales environment it's sales appointments, in an online store it might be how many people visit your website and the list goes on.

Then you need to know what happens when people have contact with your business. In other words when a customer walks in or talks with your sales personnel, what happens next...?

2. What happens when you make contact?

Really this looks at how many times you attempt to tell your story or showcase your brand, and you're looking to see how well people engage.

In a bricks and mortar store it might involve looking at heat mapping and critical data that tells you where people go and what they pick up and put down.

In traditional sales it's how many times salespeople get all the way through their marketing script or pitch. In online retail it's how many people click on your services.

Next you need to know how this converts to actual sales, because that's going to tell you if there's something wrong with your products, your pricing, your pitch or your customer service skills.

3. The big figure - actual sales

Now we know how many people have engaged with the business and how many people have expressed an interest, let's take a look at how this converts to actual sales.

This easy-to-ascertain figure of how many items or services we have sold is critical but cannot be viewed in isolation.

It needs to be ranked against potential customers and engagement to get to the true heart of your conversion rate and the effort required to actually make a sale.

Together, these three measurements tell you important things, like:

1. How many contacts are required to make a sale
2. How many engagements are required to make a sale
3. The cost and time of making a sale
4. Whether there are things wrong in your sales chain, such as too few customer contacts, or poor sales technique.

Measuring production or delivery

The next item we go about measuring is our production/delivery process.

Clearly you need to be able to deliver the item you have promised to your client, so how long does this take, what loss do you incur in the process, and how satisfied are your clients with the final result?

The production/delivery varies from business to business but can include measuring:

- Customer wait time
- Customer satisfaction
- Customer retention
- Stock loss/spoilage
- Inventory shrinkage

These measurements are about ensuring you meet your customer's required level of satisfaction in a timely manner.

This is critical insight to have because a satisfied customer is a long-term customer, and long-term customers cost less to sell to.

Measuring cashflow

Chances are you know exactly what bills will see money going out on a regular basis.

It's a cost likely to include rent, staff, stock, advertising, insurance and more, and the value of measuring this cashflow is about more than just sales to outgoings.

If we know the revenue required we can make an educated calculation of what we have to do to cover outgoings and then make a profit.

You can also then look at this calculation in reverse. For example, if you wish to make a certain profit within a given period, you will be able to factor in expenses and then calculate the number of sales required to make that figure.

You will also be able to understand what you need to do to make those sales i.e. how many customers you need to contact, how many times you need to tell your story and how many sales will likely result.

How many customer contacts has your business had this week?
How many times have you attempted to tell your story?
How many times have you completed telling your story?
How many sales have you made?

What is this information telling you?

How long does it take you to deliver your product/service?

What losses do you incur during delivery?

What percentage of your customers are repeat clients?

What are your outgoings?

What profit do you wish to achieve this week?

Start measuring task

How many sales do you need to achieve this profit?

How many contacts do you need to have?

How many times will you need to tell your story?

Now work backwards:

Date	Contact	Attempt	Complete	Close	Sale
Total					

"Start where you are. Use what you have. Do what you can".
Arthur Ashe

Turning numbers into results

If you are counting the right things in the right way you should be able to predict when and if you will have cash at hand.

When you can see this clearly it makes the running of business easier. It allows you to set goals, go out and achieve, and be excited about the business process.

Put simply, measuring allows you to see how you can achieve your goals, attain them, and set new milestones for your business.

Achieving milestones allows the business motivation to continue and so the cycle goes on.

Remember: In life we cannot control the outcome, but we can control the actions that deliver that result

What are your numbers telling you?

Measuring gives you a critical understanding of what you're achieving in your business, allowing you to move forward.

Sometimes we set a goal and things don't go as planned, but the important factor here is to understand why. That's what key measurements allow you to do.

Provided we take the appropriate measurements, we can ascertain what's happening in our business and we can make the right changes to get back to achieving results.

Remember: The same action will achieve the same results.

Understanding the numbers

Earlier we looked at three essential KPIs that are common to every business:

- Sales (revenue)
- Production (delivery)
- Cashflow (outgoings against income)

Now let's look at what those numbers mean...

Sales

Our sales measurements focussed on three areas:

- Number of contacts made
- Engagement and how often we completely told our business story or pitched our product
- Final sales

So what did these numbers reveal? Chances are, in simplistic terms, it was one of the following:

Scenario 1

If we contacted 10 people and told our story 10 times to make 8 or more sales, we know the leads are good, the story is well told and people are interested in buying our product. To improve results, however, we need more clientele.

That means we need new people to talk to, so now we look to items like our email campaigns, advertising and social media presence to create more potential clients.

And of course all these things can be measured too, giving us an insight into what campaigns attract clients.

Scenario 2

If we contacted 10 people, managed to tell our story only 5 times, resulting in 4 sales, we have some interesting factors to ponder, including:

The quality of our sales leads - are we targeting the right people in need of our services in the first place?

Our level of customer service/engagement - how well are we telling our story?

How good are our salespeople at translating the customer's initial expectation when they walk through the door to the product they would seek to buy?

Production

Next on our list of measurements was production and delivery, looking at how well we satisfied the customer's expectation, how long they had to wait and what losses were incurred during the process.

Here's what we may have uncovered:

Scenario 1

Customers were happy to buy from us in the first place but the product or service took on average 14 days to deliver in a market where competitors can deliver in 7.

This tells us we may need more staff to complete a service quickly or more stock at hand to fulfil orders more swiftly.

Scenario 2

Customers were happy to buy from us, but the majority failed to return as repeat clientele. This tells us there is something wrong with the product delivered, or our customer service/product did not meet their expectations.

Now we need to find out why by seeking customer feedback, because something needs to change. A repeat customer is always more cost effective to a business.

These are of course simplistic scenarios and your measurements may reveal far more than this. Your initial measurements may also prompt you to more carefully monitor other areas of the business process like how well specific staff convert potential customers to sales, or how well specific products are received by clientele.

Cashflow

Although bills are one of the most predictable areas of a business, what you may discover as you look at your cashflow is that you could introduce efficiencies somewhere in the business. You might uncover the following:

Scenario 1

You're spending significant time and budget on staff training due to turnover. Now you need to look at why your staff turnover is so high and perhaps reassess the management technique or staff incentives that would encourage them to stay.

Scenario 2

You have a lot of wastage/loss/shrink. In a restaurant for example, this would be pretty clear. If you're constantly throwing out chicken, you're either ordering too much, the meal does not appeal, or you need to look at marketing it as a special.

In a shopfront this would also be clear. If you are losing a lot of stock to shoplifting or employee theft, you need to look at better security and staff training.

If you're manufacturing a product and there's significant loss due to faults or machine downtime, you need to look at how to remedy this, and the list goes on.

The bottom line

Your numbers reveal all sorts of hidden and intriguing secrets about your business, and depending on your industry there might be a few or many things to count.

The key is then understanding exactly what they're trying to tell you. If it's hard to gauge what the numbers mean, you should seek assistance to gain clarity and an accurate interpretation.

While the numbers reveal the message, the interpretation of them allows you to go from a business that's "so-so" to "sensational".

It's critical to monitor performance but even more important to accurately interpret the results.

Your numbers task

"Small opportunities are often the beginning of great achievements."

Increasing activity

Business is all about activity, completing tasks, returning phone calls, filing paperwork. But business SUCCESS is actually the focus on the right activity at the right time.

When you understand your current numbers, know your KPIs and have determined the areas for adjustment, it's time to look at increasing your activity to achieve the desired result.

"All growth depends upon activity. There is no development physically or intellectually without effort, and effort means work". Calvin Coolidge

Activity - NOUN

- ♦ the condition in which things are happening or being done
- ♦ busy or vigorous action or movement
- ♦ a thing that a person or group does or has done
- ♦ actions taken by a group in order to achieve their aims
- ♦ the degree to which something displays its characteristic property or behaviour

Positive activity is about discarding the extraneous, focussing on the goal and performing the adjustment required.

By altering the simple actions you have identified through the examination of your numbers, you should see immediate results, and chances are they will compound.

You have learnt from the results what you need to address and are motivated to tackle the task. This naturally extends to the positive actions you undertake and better results ensue.

Better results lead to further motivation and the cycle continues.

What three factors did you learn about your sales process from the numbers counted earlier?

What areas of improvement are you now going to focus on?

What three factors did you learn about your production/ delivery process last session?

What areas of improvement will you now focus on?

What three things did you learn about your cashflow?

Are there any areas for improvement here?

For example:

Goals - If you have identified your goal is ultimately to enjoy a better lifestyle you may have set the aim of opening a second shopfront. What do you need to do to make it happen?

Positive activity - Focus on increasing current shopfront sales to have capital at hand.

KPIs - To enable this you know your KPIs need to reflect a certain amount of sales each month over six months.

Positive activity - Set the KPIs that indicate your sales are reaching their targets, your staff are making contact with the people they should and this contact is converting.

Measuring and adjusting - Through measuring and adjusting you have established better training methods and marketing would assist in attracting the right leads and then converting them.

Positive activity - Implement staff training processes targeting your weak spots, employ more/fresh/different marketing methods. Measure and adjust accordingly.

The ultimate result: A clear view of where you want to be and the steps you need to take to get there, without distraction. Enthusiasm to get the job done. Results that inspire you further.

In business this entire process of goal setting, measuring, adjusting and checking your management processes will occur time and again over the years. It's the reset your business requires to move forward or onto the next stage.

Activity task

What are your top 5 goals and the 5 actions you need to take to meet them?

What are your key performance indicators to ensure you are reaching these goals?

What will you measure, or what have you already measured and what are the adjustments you'll make?

With clarity and renewed focus,
now it's time to act...

Chapter 8 - Time Management

Time management can be one of the greatest challenges for any business owner, particularly when their enterprise is enjoying growth.

If your time is not managed effectively, you can quickly find yourself overwhelmed by an array of tasks all competing for your attention on a day-to-day basis.

You might also find that the business you started with the aim of creating a lifestyle with flexibility is commanding all your energy all the time.

Equally as important, you may become so caught up in the menial tasks of running an enterprise that you don't have the capacity to work on your business and plan for its future.

In this chapter, we'll look at time management and some tools to help you manage your time effectively, delegate tasks when required, and allow you to enjoy the lifestyle you deserve as a business operator.

Your time is precious

As the old saying goes 'time is money' and as your business grows that time becomes increasingly valuable.

It also becomes more precious with the demands of your business likely to see you wearing a multitude of hats, ranging from business owner to leader to chief administrator and more.

That means this time needs to be managed effectively to allow you to:

- Work on (not just in) your business
- Enjoy the lifestyle your business was built to offer
- Have a work/life balance
- Foster a positive culture
- Reduce stress and reap the rewards of your venture

It probably comes as little surprise that business owners and entrepreneurs are highly susceptible to burnout with Harvard Business Review[3] noting they are more at risk because they tend to be 'extremely passionate about work and more socially isolated, have limited safety nets, and operate in high uncertainty'.

While that all sounds a little grim, the reality is mitigating the risk of burnout involves effectively managing both your time and your mindset.

Managing your time

Managing your time effectively is not just critical to your success as a business leader. As your business grows it will also help foster a culture of success for your team and your business.

---

3 https://hbr.org/2018/04/what-makes-entrepreneurs-burn-out

So let's look at the three essential ingredients of time management.

1. **Prioritise**

   Effective time management is all about prioritising. It involves knowing exactly what needs to be accomplished each day, in what order, to move your business forward.

   That makes a to-do list your best and most faithful friend. Each day this list should be updated and ranked so you accomplish the most critical tasks first.

2. **Set measurable goals**

   The priorities you identify each day should align with the overarching goals for your business, and these should be clearly defined and known by all members of your team.

   When you know the ultimate goals, it allows you to break tasks down into bite-sized pieces and concentrate on the tasks that move your business forward.

3. **Plan ahead**

   Working in conjunction with prioritising and achieving goals is planning. Planning allows you to understand what can reasonably be accomplished within a set time frame and then create a timeline to achieve your aim.

However, the reality is there's a Catch-22 involved in the above. If you are so busy stuck in the trenches of your business just managing the day-to-day, there's a good chance you do not have the time (at present) to look at the big planning picture.

And that's a situation that needs to be addressed using the following tools.

Tools and tips for time management

Track your time

Before you really begin to look at managing your time, it's important to understand how long tasks actually take to complete. Too often we underestimate the amount of time jobs take and the interruptions that crop up throughout the day.

That's why tracking your time is critical to time management. Using tools such as time tracking software or even just a pen and paper, examine an average day in your business and life, and look specifically at what happens when.

Then look at what can be eliminated, and what can be streamlined. Maybe you're checking emails constantly when you could turn off notifications and only check them at specific times, thereby dealing with them in bulk.

Maybe that two minutes you intend to spend checking social media actually sidetracks you for half an hour. Or maybe you need to have a set period in your day where the door to your office is closed and no interruptions are permitted.

An ideal week

In business, many of us can appreciate the challenge that comes with juggling tasks and priorities.

As business owners and operators, there's staff to look after and mentor, there is paperwork to get done, jobs to handle, and in between we also need to tend to our own family and our personal wellbeing.

That's a lot to juggle in just one week comprising only 168 hours in total.

Enter the concept of the ideal week – a philosophy that first really hit the mainstream in about 2011 and sees people account for, map and allocate their time based on what they would ideally like to get done within a realistic timeframe.

The idea of the ideal week

The idea of an ideal week is a bit like having a financial budget, but in this case you are budgeting your time and your energy.

In a nutshell, the ideal week is the perfect week you would have if you had 100 per cent control of what's happening around you. And it extends to pretty much everything, accounting for leisure time, exercise, business tasks and family life.

That means the ideal week might factor in time for the exercise you want to do, the sleep you want to get, the business tasks you need to get done and the quality time you would like to spend with your kids and other family members.

In a traditional format, each theme of the ideal week is colour-coded, so red might be allocated to work, green to family time, yellow to exercise etc.

The features of an ideal week

As mentioned, an ideal week factors in ALL the things you want to get done inside and beyond the workplace.

As part of the business component of an ideal week you might allocate:

- Specific time for returning phone calls
- Time for replying to emails
- Time for staff reviews, meetings, training, etc
- Periods of time to be spent actually on the job – managing customers, performing services or manufacturing products
- Time for marketing and managing social media
- Time spent completing paperwork

There would also likely be an allocated overflow period, where you set aside time for specific items that were more complex or time-consuming than anticipated.

On the weeks you get your time "budget" correct and no overflow work is required, this slot can be used for pure leisure or personal time.

The benefits of an ideal week

The true benefit of an ideal week is that it allows you to set priorities and goals and allocate time to do them.

In many ways this is just good planning, but what the ideal week offers as a tool is realistic time tracking and accountability. Most importantly it provides clarity of mind and less stress.

The fact the week extends beyond just work accomplishments and into personal goals allows you to set these as at least an equal priority to your business.

Meanwhile, using the concept of an ideal week over an extended period offers you insight into your most time-consuming tasks and where you might need to outsource or seek help.

Ultimately, the real benefit of an ideal week is that it helps address overwhelm – a common complaint amongst business owners that we hear more and more about each day.

It allows you to understand how your time is spent, hone each week and improve your work/life balance and productivity.

It also allows you the freedom to relax in the knowledge that everything is etched on paper and you no longer need to revisit that endless mental to-do list.

Ideal, not perfection

As a final note, the ideal week is not meant to equal instant perfection. You do not fail if you do not accomplish everything you say you will when you say you should.

Instead, the ideal week is a vehicle for lifestyle and business improvement and it's one of many ways to help get your business and work/life balance back on track.

Blocking time

Similar to the idea of an ideal week is the concept of blocking time for the tasks you need to get through in any given week.

Blocking time allows you to set non-negotiable periods of your day for specific things and, when used effectively, it can be hugely helpful in maintaining the work/life balance of business.

For example, you might block 5.30am to 6.30am for exercise, 6.30am to 8.30 for family time and getting ready, 9am to 4pm to work, and so on.

The benefit of blocking time is that it allows everyone to be on the same page when it comes to what's happening, when, and also ensures you are present in the moment and focussed on the activity at hand.

The key to blocking time, however, is being realistic and strict in your approach. That means if you are at work or at home you use that time effectively without letting other tasks infringe on that allocated space.

Start your day the night before

Many successful business operators extol the virtues of starting your day the night before. Whether it's a simple list, a detailed plan or research for the day ahead, starting your day in advance ensures you are in the zone, prepared and ready to be productive straight off the bat.

While the above tools may help you manage your time more effectively, there comes a point in every business where additional resources may be required.

So now let's look at the key indicators that it's time to bring in help...

Signs you need to hire help in your business

For many business owners the idea of either hiring someone or bringing in staff can be daunting. And due to the nature of business it's often something operators fail to plan for, instead waiting to be overwhelmed before they reach out and seek assistance.

So, before you hit that critical point, here are the tell-tale signs it's time to step up and hire help to take your business further.

You have no time

Small business may be challenging and intensive, but if you have no time for other pursuits or your family life is suffering, it's time to work smarter not harder.

Contrary to what many business people feel, bringing in help can actually make money rather than just tax your revenue, allowing you to concentrate on building a business or completing tasks in your area of expertise.

You cannot meet deadlines

If your time management is excellent, but you consistently fail to meet deadlines it's definitely time to seek help. Purely and simply, it means business demand is exceeding your ability to supply.

You're saying no to jobs

One person can only do so much. Many businesses get to a point where the operator is undertaking the maximum amount of work possible and has to turn down work. This presents the opportunity to scale up with the help of an employee, contractor and/or outsourced tasks.

The truth is if you're at maximum capacity, so is your earning potential. Bringing someone in to handle extra work allows you to grow as a business and increase the financial return.

Unable to plan for the future

Successful business is about planning and creating goals that ultimately enable the lifestyle of your choosing. In short, you need to be captaining your ship, not frantically rowing in circles or constantly bailing out water.

If you're busy, but stuck in a holding pattern that won't allow you to plan, you need to look at delegating tasks.

Too much time on jobs that others could do

Yes, small business requires the wearing of many hats, but chances are you're spending too much time on jobs others could do.

Look at the jobs you do each day and account for them. How much time is spent on administrative tasks that someone else could easily do like invoicing, answering the phone or fiddling around with your website?

These are the first areas you can either outsource or bring someone in to handle.

Enthusiasm is dwindling

Small business is a job, and chances are some days it inspires you more than others. But if you feel like you never have free time and all your days are spent playing catchup, it's hard to maintain passion for your enterprise.

Before you reach the point where that enthusiasm totally wanes, bring in the assistance you need so you feel like you're on top of tasks and your business is going somewhere.

Quick ways to get the help you need

- Outsource tasks to experts like website managers, bookkeepers etc.
- Hire a virtual assistant or freelancer for admin tasks
- Bring in an administrative assistant part-time or permanently to handle a variety of small tasks.
- Bring in a co-worker or contractor to do some of the core jobs that you do
- Bring in permanent staff
- Consider software that streamlines mundane repetitive tasks

When to bring on staff

In every business' growth journey there comes a point where additional resources and investment will be required.

At this critical juncture, it's likely you, the business operator, are working at capacity, it's a struggle to complete all the small business tasks required, and there simply aren't enough hours in the day to get everything done.

At this stage, it's also likely you have maxed out your earning potential under your current business model.

And, it might sound obvious, but this is the point where you will need to bring in staff if you want your business to grow.

So what are the signs your business is ready to bring on staff?

You're no longer doing what your best at

As the owner of a business, chances are your natural talent and passion is dollar-productive activity, such as providing a service, finding new clients or producing something.

In a growing business, there comes a point where you are likely to be waylaid by the other tasks that business operation requires, such as invoicing, accounts receivable, marketing and more.

These are tasks you should be delegating so you can get back to what you do best.

Work backlogs

Whether it's a backlog of orders or you are knocking back customers seeking your services, when the workload outstrips your ability to cater properly to your clientele, now is the time to look at bringing in help.

Sales is not your strength

This might sound counterintuitive, but every business relies on sales and sometimes the business owner is not the best salesperson.

While they know what they want their business to achieve, and they also know there is customer demand for the product, they're just not comfortable conveying the value of a product or service to the world.

If this sounds like you, it might be time to bring in a salesperson who is skilled in this area, and the growth results might be well worth the investment.

You have maxed out your earning potential

There are only so many hours in a day and the reality is you can only fulfil so many orders and complete a set number of services each week.

If you've hit this capacity, you have also maxed out your current earning potential, unless you decide to increase the price of your product.

But in most cases, this is the stage where you bring people in to increase your business output and enjoy additional revenue.

You have made a growth decision

One major reason to bring in staff is because you have made a strategic growth decision. You want to expand your business, and the only way to do that is with additional resources.

If any of the above factors sound familiar, it's likely you are ready to bring in staff, but there are a few things your business should have in place before that occurs.

For a brief overview, you can visit the Australian Government's staff checklist at **https://business.gov.au/people/employees/ hiring-employees.**

Tips for tech that streamlines your operation

In this day and age there is a wealth of technology available to streamline your operation and save you valuable time.

In the process it can make your job as a business leader easier, allow for transparency across your enterprise, and also create better efficiency and productivity in your team.

From Customer Relationship Management software to workflow apps, and social media automation tools, some of these products can make a real difference to how your business operates, allowing you to streamline tasks and offer better service.

That said, the world of business technology can be a noisy space, with bright, shiny new products consistently hitting the market.

Choosing the right technology or gauging whether the latest product is right for you can also be overwhelming.

So, regardless of what the latest offering is, here are some tips on analysing tech for your business.

Tech in the context of business

Often when clients and I are discussing future plans and growth for their business, we consider the role technology could play in streamlining their existing operation.

After all, the right technology has the ability to free a business operator of repetitive administration tasks so they can direct their energy towards expansion or the big business picture.

It can also assist with the systems and procedures that drive the inner workings of a business, ensuring service is consistent, standards are met and staff know exactly what they should be doing.

But drawing on technology isn't about deploying tech tools for the sake of it or because a new buzzword is making the rounds in your industry.

Instead, it should be considered within the context of your specific business, and measured against the following questions...

Does it solve a problem?

Any bright shiny new tech tool you embrace for your business should solve a very specific problem that you have identified.

That problem can be business-related or customer-related but knowing the problem you need to address allows you to identify the tech features that you need.

Ultimately, the tool will then allow you to improve areas like customer service, or productivity and business efficiency.

Will it allow me to focus on more important areas?

Technology might allow you to automate and streamline, but in the process it should also allow you to focus on more important areas, such as human connections and customer interaction.

Occasionally there's a danger of businesses deploying so much technology and using it so frequently that the human connection and personalisation is lost.

So, ensure your use of tech isn't just about removing tasks, but also then enables you to replace those mundane repetitive jobs with high-value touchpoints that better service your customer.

Is it user friendly?

The technology you do embrace should be user friendly for you as the business leader and your team. That means considering how easy it is to adopt, how much maintenance it will require and whether it's scalable, should your business grow.

Is it cost effective?

Any tech tool should be considered within your business plan and budget. It's all very well to want the latest software and technology, but be mindful the aim of any technology salesperson is to attempt to justify the cost involved.

You need to weigh this cost carefully against projected benefits to your specific business in terms of productivity, savings and efficiency or the value it offers to the customer experience.

Making time to work on, not just in, your business

In this chapter our prime focus has been time management in a bid to help you use your time more effectively and productively each day.

This is partly to ensure you avoid burnout, maintain the work life balance and accomplish all the tasks you need to. But it's also about providing time for you to work on, not just in your business.

When you work on your business, planning for the future and developing strategies for growth, you are moving your business forward.

So now, let's focus specifically on ensuring you have the time to work on, not just in your business and you use that time wisely.

Make time

Every business owner should be setting aside a specific block of time to work on their business – whether that involves examining and questioning the figures, setting goals, planning, or revising policy.

In theory that sounds easy, but as any business operator will tell you, this time often falls by the wayside when other, more immediate 'dollar productive' tasks pop up.

In other words, it's easy to defer going through your figures when the opportunity to quote on a new project or actually complete a job arises.

The important thing to remember here is that working on your business builds income for the long run, positioning you where you want to be in the future, while working in your business meets an immediate need right now.

So how do you resolve these two opposing business elements?

Consider it an investment

Although it might be hard to quantify in dollar terms, it's critical to recognise that planning, revising and preparing are actually income producing tasks – you just don't tend to see the results immediately.

Instead, these tasks are an investment in your business. So factor it into your business costs and allocate sufficient time within the working week when you essentially pay yourself for your expert business insight.

Delegate

If you're finding you do not have the time to work on your business due to interruptions or the fact you are on the job, it's time to look at delegating the more menial tasks during set periods.

Is there someone else in your business who could handle incoming phone calls for an hour? Could you outsource the invoicing? Is there software that might make your work more efficient, so you have a little time to spare?

Make it part of your routine

Whether it's Friday afternoon, or first thing Monday morning, block time in your calendar and stick to it. This is a period when you are unavailable to take calls, answer emails, schedule meetings or see staff. Unless it is an emergency, this block of time is non-negotiable.

Remember it doesn't have to be a whole day. Even just an hour a week starts to add up when it comes to working on where you want your business to go.

Have your files and notes accessible

There's no point spending half of your allotted planning time seeking out the documents you need and looking for notes you have previously taken.

Have a dedicated folder, drawer, shelf or file where your business planning information resides. Keep this information separate from other tasks so you can easily come back to it and pick up where you left off previously.

Keep the big picture front of mind

Working on your business allows it to build momentum over time. It enables you to chart where you want to go personally and professionally then set goals and meet them.

It's about the big-picture not the fine print, and when you keep that front of mind and make working on your business a habit, you will find you have greater clarity and an improved ability to take your business where you want it to go.

Chapter 9 - Leadership

Whether you envisaged it or not when you first started in business, any business owner is the captain at the helm of a ship.

In this role you are not only responsible for your own financial welfare but the livelihood of others, their job satisfaction and the course that your boat will navigate to reach the sunny shores of success.

For some this leadership comes easily, for others the waters are murky and unfamiliar, but great leadership can be the difference between a rough and arduous voyage and smooth sailing in the business world.

Here are three keys to great leadership...

The destination

If you don't know the destination, then how do you set sail?

Like any journey on the high seas, business is about knowing where you want to go and how to get there.

But it's also about taking precautionary measures and altering course when the weather gets rough or you no longer have the wind at your back.

Leadership style

Every captain has a method to galvanise their crew and every leader a leadership style, but often it's hard to hold up the mirror and ascertain exactly what that is.

Ultimately the best leaders are self aware; they know when to encourage, when to challenge, when to reward and when to course-correct.

Every leader should evaluate their techniques to ascertain what works and what does not to ensure they are leading with strength and respect.

Know your team

Behind every great leader is an equally excellent team. Harmonious and successful workplaces see each member of that team playing to their strengths.

As the owner of the business you should know how each member of your crew works, and be aware of their strengths and weaknesses.

Staff should be trained in their roles, given the right tools to do their job, and provided with feedback.

This includes providing clear job descriptions and recognising team members who do their job well.

Ultimately, great leaders are masters at the 'art of people', knowing how to direct and maneuvre their crew, and the direction in which to take them.

Know your leadership style

Regardless of whether your leadership skills came to you organically or through learning, most business leaders embrace one of six distinct leadership styles.

There's also a decent chance you have more than one approach, depending on the circumstances.

Meanwhile, research further indicates some leadership styles work better than others when it comes to building morale and also depending on the job that needs to get done and the timeframe in which you are operating.

So, let's examine the 'six leadership styles' and those which have been found to serve managers best.

The authoritative leader

Considered the most effective leader of all, the authoritative leader offers a combination of support, confidence and vision.

They are a leader for the future, understanding their staff may need to take calculated risks in order to learn, grow and offer ideas beyond those of their competition.

With the big picture as the focus, the authoritative leader commands the respect of staff, while the strategy works particularly well when businesses are looking to embrace a new vision or achieve different results.

Although this leadership style has few downsides, the person using it must be sufficiently knowledgeable and charismatic. They must be able to propel people towards a greater idea, while fostering the strengths of their own team members.

They must also tread the fine line between knowledgeable and overbearing.

The democratic leader

The democratic leader achieves through consensus, seeking the opinion of their team and involving them in the vision of a business.

With the catchphrase 'What do you think?', they believe in having their team invested emotionally in an organisation.

This strategy is renowned for building morale, motivating groups and achieving results as a cohesive unit. It is considered most effective when used to endorse a plan or when driving a team to embrace a new vision.

However, under severe time constraints, this leadership style can become impractical.

The coaching leader

With the mantra 'Try this', the coaching leader helps build the skills of their team using their experience to achieve success.

The coaching leader is considered available to their staff, supportive and focussed on the future. They look to build a team's skillset and experience as part of an investment in their company's future.

The coaching leader is also likely an excellent delegator, identifying the skills and weaknesses in each team member and working to create a cohesive unit.

This is a leader with the future at the forefront of their mind, however their strategy takes time to implement, and requires receptiveness and self-motivation of each team member in order to make progress.

The affiliative leader

The affiliative leader is one who praises and nurtures their team into performance, with the belief 'people come first'.

Their ethos involves creating harmony and an emotional bond with staff in order to better motivate employees.

Considered one of the best leadership approaches, the affiliative leader has a focus on overall team morale, nurturing each member as part of a cohesive unit.

On the downside, an overly friendly and nurturing leader can create a culture where poor performance is tolerated, or where constructive criticism isn't effectively used.

Although highly effective, the affiliative leadership style often works best when employed alongside other leadership traits.

The pacesetting leader

The pacesetting leader sets high standards that they expect their team to follow. With the catchphrase 'follow me', this is a leadership method that should be used with caution.

Often the pacesetting leader's standards are hard for their team to read or attain, which can ultimately result in staff becoming overwhelmed, losing morale or simply giving up.

On the positive side, a pacesetting leader can quickly achieve results. At their best they may be considered firm but fair and are leaders who offer expertise through example.

The coercive leader

This type of leader demands compliance with the belief their team members should 'do what I tell you'.

While considered a useful style in a crisis or when attempting to turn around the behaviour of an employee as a last resort, the coercive leader may struggle to create a team environment, instead believing subjects will simply obey.

In fact, the coercive leader is one considered to have the most potential negative impact on an organisation's culture.

Culture shock – Why culture is critical in business

You can talk growth, vision, business mindset and numbers, but one often underestimated asset of the most successful businesses is culture.

This near unquantifiable X-factor is all about the team ethos. Get it right, you attract great staff and great customers. Get it wrong and your business can be a minefield of poor service, staff personality clashes, and lagging morale.

So, what is culture, why is it critical to business and how do you set yourself up for a positive workplace?

Culture by definition

As Harvard Business Review[4] notes: "Culture is the tacit social order of an organisation".

"It shapes attitudes and behaviours in wide-ranging and durable ways. Cultural norms define what is encouraged, discouraged, accepted, or rejected within a group".

Importantly, culture manifests in different ways. It is reflected in the way your team works together, the way they speak to and about each other, and the service provided to your customers.

In other words, it is "felt" at every level of an organisation, including by the customers who engage with your business.

Why culture is critical

Unfortunately, many of us can relate to the concept of a toxic workplace culture, because at some point in our career there's a likelihood we've experienced it first-hand.

This is the type of environment where bullying and harassment hide in plain sight and where staff morale is low.

As a result, staff members rarely take joy in their workplace and

---

[4] https://hbr.org/2018/01/the-leaders-guide-to-corporate-culture

its duties and the customer experience suffers.

On the flipside, a positive business culture is linked to happier employees who are also more efficient, provide better service, take greater ownership of their responsibilities, and are more productive.

This in turn translates to the customer experience.

So how do you instil a positive business culture?

How to shape a positive business culture

Leadership

A positive business culture starts at the top, with a conscientious leader who is clear on what the company hopes to achieve, and the behaviour their business seeks to espouse.

This leader will also be clear on the type of people they are looking to build their business with in terms of the staff they hire, the behaviour they expect and the attitude they reward.

Critically, the leader will need to practise what they preach when it comes to culture, espousing the values of their business and acting as a role model in terms of that behaviour and attitude.

Vision

The business culture then translates to staff through the company's vision as well as its hiring practices, systems and procedures.

This acts as the written framework a business culture operates within.

Staff

Staff are critical to any company culture, which is why it's imperative not just to have staff who fulfil required duties, but also have an ethos that aligns with a company's values.

Occasionally, that may mean forgoing a 'top performer' and instead hiring the near top performer who has a better attitude.

As the culture of a business becomes apparent, like-minded people, including staff and clientele, are more likely to be attracted to that business.

Training

Solid training, career opportunities and a growth mindset are often interlinked with a positive business culture.

This focus on growth and opportunity allows staff to develop in their position, take calculated risks, and learn from any mistakes, while engendering loyalty and job satisfaction.

Communication

Key to any positive workplace culture is clear communication. This includes updates on company progress, shared ownership of projects and ideas, and an open-door policy that nips any potential issues in the bud.

Accountability

Within a positive workplace culture there will also be a focus on accountability that allows staff to take ownership of their actions and their career path.

For the leader, this also involves holding staff accountable to their commitments, and includes building people up but identifying and addressing negative behaviour.

Culture is key

Culture is a key component of business success. Positive business cultures attract good people, recognise effort and performance and in turn this translates to the experience for the customer.

The fact of the matter is this, culture also impacts the business bottom line. Why?

Because statistics indicate companies with highly engaged employees outperform their competitors by 147 per cent, while businesses that excel at customer experience have 1.5 times more engaged employees than companies with a record of poor customer experience.

Managing your mindset

Your business mindset is basically the way you think about your business. It is recognition that how you mentally approach business and its challenges has an impact on your likelihood of success.

This success includes how your brand is perceived, the services and products you offer, the leadership of your staff, and the processes you embrace to get where you want to go.

There are different types of business mindsets, including growth and fixed, but the critical takeaway is that your attitude will impact your business, particularly during periods of challenge and change.

Top mindset tools to embrace

Managing your business mindset is a bit like shifting gears on a car. It's akin to taking your business out of neutral, where it might be coasting or have stalled, and putting it into first, second, third or fourth gear with a clear destination in sight.

To do that the following tools may assist...

The road ahead, not the rearview mirror

While it's important to acknowledge your previous business journey, dwelling on the past won't get you where you want to go in the future.

An empowered business mindset sees you firmly focussed on what needs to happen next, drawing on the wisdom gained through mistakes and achievements of the past.

Believe you'll succeed

The most important thing to realise and hold firm in your mind is that you have the power to reach your business destination. You will succeed.

You will do so using similar tools to the ones that saw you start an enterprise in the first place and a few new ones you have developed along the way.

Know your why

Now is the time to very clearly define the why behind your business, including what you are looking to offer others and what your business should offer you. In other words, why do you get up in the morning and open that business door?

Knowing your why and keeping it front of mind allows you to maintain business motivation. Sharing that why with your staff also keeps them energised and engaged.

Understand mistakes are opportunities

This speaks to the growth mindset that many business owners and entrepreneurs look to embrace. When you understand mistakes are opportunities to learn and evolve, you free yourself and your business to keep reaching for the stars.

On that note, actively pursue learning, to arm yourself with new tools and insight that motivate and encourage you and your business to move forward.

Develop daily habits

Daily habits have long been linked to both personal and business success. They take much of the mundane thinking out of the business landscape, allowing processes to occur effortlessly at a set time.

When developing daily habits, look to what works for you and your business, then stick to them.

These daily habits might be different for every business and every individual but might include a workout at 7am before a business day that starts with half an hour of returning emails, or a daily routine of making calls between 9am and 9.30am before processing orders and doing paperwork.

Know your process

You know what works for your business and what doesn't. At this point that may require a little revision, but process should be at the heart of what you do.

When it comes to running your business and decision making, your processes allow you to move forward quickly without overthinking the little things.

Involve your team

Once you've spent time cultivating your business mindset, be sure to involve your team by clearly outlining the planned path forward.

When you engage the team around you, you inspire passion, confidence and loyalty, allowing you to ramp up and bring the best out of the staff as you collectively look to the road ahead.

Sharing the business journey with staff

They're the people in the trenches with you, the ones facing the customer, completing the tasks and putting a face to your business name.

Staff can make or break a business, but the truth is in most instances your management technique can make or break them.

Here are five tips for setting up great staff dynamics and bringing them along for your business ride.

Clear position descriptions

From the moment you consider taking on a new staff member your focus should be clear communication.

This starts in the form of written position descriptions so a potential employee knows exactly what their role entails. Position descriptions include responsibilities, entitlements and who they are answerable to.

This sets up a dynamic of professionalism and clarity, and is a document that can be referred to when required.

Training

At the outset, training, including induction programs, should be part of your management process.

Comprehensive initial and ongoing training allows a business owner to establish their preferred operating methods and arm staff with the tools to do their job.

More than that, it indicates an investment in staff that makes them feel valued.

Policies and procedures

Supporting any training should be documents that outline how the business operates in the form of policies and procedures.

These 'how-to' guides for the day-to-day running of a business give a big-picture perspective of who's responsible for what tasks, what to do when things don't go to plan, and establish the ethos of a business.

A copy should be provided to staff when they commence employment, and be readily available in the office.

Policies and procedures should also be regularly updated and staff should be educated about their contents.

Reviews and feedback

One of the best ways to have staff feel accountable and valued is through regular feedback and reviews.

Verbal feedback should be timely, clear, concise, calm, sincere and relevant.

And it's not a one-way street. By encouraging your staff to provide feedback to you with an open door communication policy, you enable them to air their feelings, solve problems and enjoy being a valued contributor.

Formal reviews like performance appraisals should be undertaken at least once a year with reference to the position description and any further criteria you have established.

As a manager, take the time to write specific notes and plan what you have to say in advance.

This is also a good opportunity to ask an employee what they would like to achieve in your business in the future.

Rewards

Rewards, such as annual bonuses or gifts that recognise a job well done, go a long way to expressing your appreciation for a team or staff member who has consistently lived up to or exceeded your expectations.

Something as simple as a little extra in the pay packet after a time-consuming product launch makes your staff feel valued and appreciated, fostering good morale.

Communication and the art of listening

In business, we often fall back on phrases like talking the talk, nailing the elevator pitch, mastering the sales spiel, and honing the marketing message.

But while the information you have to offer is important to your business and your brand, so too are the nuggets of wisdom served up by your clientele and your staff.

That means 'listening' in business is just as important as 'speaking'. Because when we listen, we begin to understand the customer needs, their purchasing hesitation and how we can improve our offering.

Here's an insight into the art of listening and how it serves your business in a host of different ways.

"Most of the successful people I've known are the ones who do more listening than talking." - Bernard Baruch

Times change, trends come and go, so how can a business keep its finger on the fast-changing pulse? Through listening - in a variety of ways.

From listening to the customer for their feedback and complaints, to hearing what your staff have to say about what's working in a business and what is not, listening allows us to better comprehend the playing field in which our business operates.

Listening is also essential to selling. It allows us to comprehend a consumer's problem and identify the way to solve it via a business' products or service.

Meanwhile, listening can take many forms - it can be proactive, incidental, simple or an activity you need to engage in.

"Wisdom is the reward you get for a lifetime of listening when you'd have preferred to talk." - Doug Larson

Listening can be as simple as seeking feedback from customers on social media or asking your staff how it's going, to better understand the issues they face.

It can be complex, involving deciphering the underlying message in feedback you prefer to not hear.

It can be proactive, as part of a team identifying new concepts, or it can be formal as part of the processes and procedures you use to manage your staff and your customer service.

Importantly, listening can involve identifying the things we don't hear but believe we should when people talk about our business.

Simple listening

"What do you think?" is one of the most insightful questions any business owner can ask; both of their customers and their staff.

By asking the opinion of others, a business can learn the ways to improve their service or offering, and what's missing in the market they cater to.

But it's not seeking the opinion of just anyone that matters - it's asking for the informed feedback of your ideal customers and your trusted frontline staff.

These are the people who have a vested interest in your business and its future. These are the people to whom your products and services apply.

Formal listening

Listening can also be formal - it can be a well-posed question during an annual staff performance review or actively seeking testimonials and survey responses from customers.

It can involve compiling the feedback you receive and then creating the strategies that meet a new demand or address an issue.

Proactive listening

In business, listening can also be proactive. It can be the brainstorming session you have with your staff to identify new initiatives and solutions. It can be the product testing you commission or the consumer panel you invite to review and provide feedback on a product or service.

"When you talk, you are only repeating what you already know. But if you listen, you may learn something new." Dalai Lama

Regardless of whether it's proactive or incidental, listening is critical to business success and occasionally it's a skill that needs to be learned.

True listening is an activity. It requires you to set aside preconceptions, clear your mind of distractions and really hear what the speaker has to say.

Often that listening will also include deciphering and clarifying what the speaker means rather than just absorbing the exact words they offer.

It may also involve determining and accepting the truth within a message you may not wish to hear.

But regardless, listening indicates your business is committed to being better. It also ensures your customers and staff are welcome, respected and invested in your future and with you for the inevitable ups, downs and improvements that are the hallmarks of any successful business ride.

Seven traits of successful small business owners

Small businesses and the industries they represent may differ widely, but often the traits of those who lead them are remarkably similar.

In over 30 years of business coaching here are the seven character traits that stand out in the small business owners I've encountered who achieve success...

Driven

It takes drive and passion to start an enterprise then lead it year after year, day in day out, and those who do it best possess these traits in spades.

It's the drive to see things differently, assess the risks, take a gamble and learn from mistakes that stems from a vision to achieve beyond the average.

Goal-oriented

Business is about vision and goals – the vision of a unique offering and successful operation, the goal of a better life, a solid income, of six staff instead of two.

Successful operators not only establish goals but stick to them, assessing their effectiveness, relevance and outcome. And it's not just the big goals like increased revenue, it's short term goals that equate to major success when compounded over time.

Organised

Think small business and it's all about keeping lots of balls in the air. It's about payroll, accounts payable, marketing, stock and products, which makes successful operators adept at multi-tasking.

They know their time is money and that they must account for it, save it and value it while ensuring business does not engulf their entire life.

The best operators are strict with their time, allocating it to the various tasks required.

Creative

Creativity isn't just about an entrepreneurial spirit, it extends to problem solving, customer knowledge, sensing opportunity, and having the ability to work through an issue by seeing it differently.

Resilient

There are few small businesses which have a completely easy ride. There will always be times of challenge, changing trends, new competition or economic slumps, but successful operators see this as part of the journey. Many view a challenge as an opportunity to learn and evolve, shift gears and set new goals.

They will upskill when required, seek help when necessary and step back to take a different view of their business.

Confident

When you're at the helm of a ship you require an inherent confidence in your ability to reach the destination you choose. This is a quiet confidence, not arrogance, in your ability to create a vision, set goals, hire the right people and lead them well.

It's also a confidence that you know what your customer wants and can deliver it with consistency.

Humble

This may seem like a direct contradiction to confidence, but in truth the two go hand in hand.

Success is often about the confidence and humility to recognise when you need help, when you require better expertise or should seek advice to move forward. It's about recognising mistakes and having the awareness to analyse them, learn from them and use them as part of your arsenal of business skills.

Chapter 10 - Handling the tough stuff

As rewarding as having your own business might be, it comes with its fair share of challenges.

At any given time these challenges may range from staffing issues, to culture problems, negative feedback from customers, and troublesome clients.

In this chapter we'll look at handling the tough stuff of business, in the knowledge that while it may feel like a huge hurdle at the time, overcoming challenge is actually par for the course of being in business...it's all about perspective.

Staffing issues

As the face of your business, your staff can be both your greatest asset and your biggest weak spot.

That makes selecting the right staff imperative, while they must be onboarded into your business properly as well.

But what happens when there are issues with your staff in the form of personalities that clash, or people who simply don't deliver what they promised?

Well then things get tricky, so let's explore some of the more common staffing issues and how to solve them.

Too many staff versus too few

Staffing requires a careful balance. Too many staff will see your business losing profit to an excessive payroll. Too few staff will result in your existing employees feeling stressed and will result in lost productivity.

So how do you find the right balance? Well, staffing requires planning. You should forecast what roles need to be filled in your business long before a vacancy starts to have an input on work output, and you should proactively consider what skills that employee needs to bring to the table.

Your staffing forecast should be part of your business plan, taking into account busy periods within a business when casuals might be required, or jobs that might be outsourced externally to contractors.

Quality

The quality of your staff affects the quality of your customer service and your business' productivity.

If your business is growing, you should have a recruitment policy in place that allows you to find the right people to suit the culture and skills required in your business.

This policy will include information on:

- How and where you source staff
- The interview process
- Reference checking process

- Job descriptions for each important role within your business
- A culture playbook of what's expected within your business and what your business stands for
- Onboarding procedures and checklists
- Training manuals
- Workplace Health and Safety requirements
- Staff reviews and feedback procedures

Staff stress

Staff stress is becoming an issue that is discussed more and more frequently within business circles.

If your staff are stressed, they will be less productive, have lower morale and also have decreased job satisfaction which is likely to lead to a higher turnover of employees.

Mitigating staff stress includes:

- Having an open door policy so any problems can be discussed before they become issues
- Scheduling regular time off and required leave for your staff
- Ensuring key roles in your business are filled by the right people
- Rewarding staff members for a job well done
- Ensuring your staff have the tools and ability to switch off at the end of the day

Personality conflicts

Although they're not fun to deal with, occasionally there will be staff conflicts within any business.

But mitigating them involves having clear policies on expected staff behaviour, hiring people to fit the culture of your business, and maintaining a workplace with a positive, collaborative and professional focus.

Meanwhile, good communication is the key to nipping any staff conflicts in the bud, whether that's through an open door policy, regular team meetings, or group goal setting.

An essential ingredient of business success

Ultimately staffing issues are one of the most important factors to address within any business. Get it wrong and morale within your organisation will plummet. Get it right and you will have a team that seamlessly works together to ensure your business success.

Culture crisis

At some point in our career most of us have worked with a toxic staff member. And if you've had that misfortune, you are well and truly aware of the damage just one person can cause when it comes to culture and morale in a business.

But what should the business leader do if there's a toxic staff member in their ranks? Well, in short, you can never just turn a blind eye

Here's an insight into the legacy of toxic staff members and the steps a business leader should take to address their behaviour.

What is a toxic staff member?

The toxic staff member can come in a number of guises. They might be the person who constantly moans about everything... absolutely everything.

They might also be someone who quietly undermines other staff members or perhaps takes credit for achievements which are not theirs to claim.

They might consistently behave badly, yelling at others, blaming or even quietly bullying.

On the flipside, the toxic staff member might also be your best performer, but it's their arrogance and indifference to others that has a lasting impact on your whole team.

However, make no mistake, if there's a toxic staff member in your midst, the impacts can be long-lasting.

The effect of a toxic staff member

The impacts of a toxic staff member can be far reaching. Their attitude and behaviour can seep into the morale of every member of your team.

Ultimately a toxic staff member can damage your company culture and their behaviour might directly cause other valued staff members to leave.

But how can you tell if you have a toxic staff member on your team?

How do you identify a toxic staff member?

Your other staff are the best clue as to whether there's a toxic staff member in your midst. The signs might be subtle at first, with staff illustrating an unwillingness to work with that person.

It might be as simple as one person always being in the right place at the right time to take credit for a team's achievements.

They might also be more overt, with other team members mentioning their behaviour. That's why it's important to have an open-door policy in any business, so small team issues can be nipped in the bud, and less than desirable behaviour can be swiftly addressed.

What do you do?

Toxicity in your staff ranks is something that cannot be ignored.

After all, the behaviour you walk past is the behaviour you accept.

The first step is to address that behaviour in the moment, by pulling the staff member aside and asking them what prompted their actions.

That includes taking an interest in how they are and what's going on in their world.

This should be a private discussion, because in workplaces with a positive culture, a leader will ideally praise in public but question in private.

Then it's about engaging the staff member and coming up with a strategy to change that behaviour - without judgement and with the belief that the staff member is capable of better.

As part of this you could perhaps set a timeframe for actions that will address that behaviour as well. But the staff member needs to be a core part of that strategy as that indicates they recognise the behaviour that impacts others.

Sometimes toxicity needs to be cut loose

Occasionally, toxic behaviour is so ingrained that the best way to address a staff member's actions is to cut that staff member loose.

After all, the impacts of a negative staff member have such widespread impacts that the cost to your culture, business and other staff members simply isn't worth it.

Meanwhile, it's critical for the culture of your entire team that negative behaviour needs to be seen to be addressed.

A leadership question

The final question to ask yourself as a leader is: 'Have you allowed a workplace where this type of behaviour is permissible?' and that speaks to the core values of your culture and your hiring practices.

Toxic staff members can curb a business in a variety of ways. They can prohibit other staff members from shining, stop a team from performing at their best, and cost you real money in terms of staff churn and customer loyalty – not to mention the unease, anxiety and stress you are likely to experience.

Troublesome clients

Staff might be the face of your business, but clients are the reason your enterprise exists, and occasionally they too come with their own challenges, not all of which you can solve.

So let's look at a couple of potential issues that might arise when it comes to managing clients...

Signs it's time to split with a client

In business, the aim is to find and keep a client, right? Well yes, and very occasionally no.

What if the relationship with a specific client is no longer serving the needs of your business, comes at the expense of better clientele, or worse still, is actually costing you time and money?

As much as we might hate to let a long-term client go, there are occasions when the need arises in the interests of your business and even for your personal wellbeing.

Here are four signs it's time to part ways with a client, and how to cut them loose with minimal pain...

A client audit

Just as a business audits its finances, its stock and considers its staff needs each year, they should be conducting an audit of their clients.

This audit is based on key metrics along with some criteria that's harder to measure. Clients should be considered on what they bring into a business, how reliable they are at paying, and quite simply how you feel about dealing with them.

It's important to note, like a business itself, the type of clients you have will evolve over time. Often start-up businesses will bring clients on board because they feel they need them. That may mean they go above and beyond to serve this initial client in the interests of building a reputation.

While they are finding their feet, they might also charge less than they should, or fail to establish the right boundaries.

Two or three years later, however, that playing field has likely changed. You clearly know the sweet spot when it comes to pricing your products or services, understand the value you bring, and know exactly what constitutes a good client or one who is slightly more painful.

But if you're looking for clear indicators it's time to let go, here are the top four signs.

They're paying you less than you're worth

Each year a business should evaluate its pricing. In many cases it will need to rise in line with CPI or the quality of services and products you deliver. However, often a client audit will reveal a number who have been paying below market price.

In a few cases, that might be OK because of the other benefits they deliver to your business like on-time payments, prestige, referrals etc.

But in others, the time, effort and resources you dedicate to this client are a legacy of the past. If these clients are not willing to pay for your services at your current market price then they are costing you time, effort and resources that would be better utilised elsewhere.

They're taking too much of your time

In business and life there will always be people who you give an inch to and they take a mile. If you're going above and beyond for a client, chasing invoices, or constantly working to please a hard-to-satisfy client, it's time to cut them loose.

There are better areas and better clients to apply your energy to.

They're treating you poorly

No relationship with a client should come at the expense of your self-esteem or mental wellbeing. If you're being treated poorly via rude emails, ridiculous demands or a failure to pay when they should, this is the top indicator a client needs to go.

Yes, you're in business and customer satisfaction is key, but in the real-world there is a limit of what you need to endure.

And if fear of poor reviews or bad word of mouth is holding you back, don't let it. Potential clientele can spot an aberration amongst otherwise positive testimonials from a mile away.

You're not delivering what you feel you should

In the early stages of business, you might say yes to jobs that are a little outside what you really wish to be known for. Meanwhile, some clients might employ you for your expertise but then fail to listen to it.

On a further note, there might be some jobs that you simply lack enthusiasm for because of one or all the factors above, and you find this lack of passion means the work you produce doesn't live up to your own expectations.

These are all clear indicators this might be a client to shed.

What to do?

Breaking up is never easy, and don't underestimate the very

real fear it can elicit in business. However, often losing a client in the interests of better serving others can open new doors of opportunity, allowing you to concentrate on the areas that matter, and improve your income.

If you're considering making the split, do it cleanly and professionally.

- Clearly understand the reasons why the break needs to be made
- Remove emotion from the equation
- Politely indicate the reasons behind your decision
- Appreciate their side of things – most clients understand a working relationship should be a win-win situation
- Give them sufficient notice
- Offer them a referral to another who you feel may better suit their needs

You'd be surprised at the relief that comes with losing a client who is not serving your business needs, and chances are you have better clients out there who you can now focus your attention on to build your business.

The reality is, bringing on and shedding clients is a normal part of business. It indicates you're growing, evolving and improving over time.

Outstanding invoices - Are you a business or a charity?

Outstanding invoices – whether you're a small business or large, they're the bugbear of most organisations.

Money that is owed to you as a business is cash that you do not have at your disposal, income you have not yet earned, and a liability too many businesses willingly shoulder.

So, let's talk about outstanding invoices, their impact, and the thinking in your business that needs to change...

Some cold hard stat's

We all know the statistic that 60 per cent of small businesses fail within their first three years of operation in Australia.

Most of us appreciate lack of market research, poor management, and lack of planning play a role.

But an equally likely candidate is poor cash management, and that's not just about expenditure, it's about the income you fail to collect as well.

Statistics from 2017[5] indicated Australian businesses were collectively owed $76 billion in outstanding invoices, meaning an average business could have around $38,000 owed to them by customers.

As that's almost akin to a full-time starting wage, that's no small figure to overlook.

The trouble with outstanding invoices

The trouble with outstanding invoices is they affect your cashflow which goes on to impact your ability to grow, to employ extra staff and to enjoy the lifestyle which you believed your business would offer.

In fact, a recent SME cash flow crisis report by the Invoice Market[6] found cash flow is so dire for 38 per cent of Australian small businesses that owners dip into their personal savings to manage their company finances.

This in turn impacts their ability to pay their housing and other living expenses.

And it begs the question, why do we let it get so bad?

[5] https://www.adviservoice.com.au/2017/01/small-business-cash-flow-crisis-costing-australian-economy-76-billion/
[6] https://insidesmallbusiness.com.au/management/planning-management/small-business-cashflow-crisis-costing-australian-economy-76-billion

The five biggest mistakes you probably make

Poor invoice management comes down to a range of factors, not least of which are the systems and procedures you adopt behind the scenes, and the mindset you embrace when it comes to customer relations.

So here I'll outline the five biggest mistakes.

1.   **Your customers are not your friends**

      You may like them, you may work well with them, but your customers are not your friends – they engage you for a service or product for which they expect to pay.

2.   **You fail to be clear from the outset**

      All businesses should have strict terms and conditions when it comes to payments. These should be obvious in your quotes, in your invoicing, and in the policies and procedures within your business.

3.   **Your invoicing is sloppy**

      This is a similar point to the last one, but take a moment to consider how regularly you invoice, and how much time elapses between the sale of a product or service and when the invoice for it goes out.

      Every business should have a strict system that ensures invoices go out as soon as possible to ensure you get paid on time.

      If that's proving too great a task for you as the business owner, it's time to automate or call in some help.

4.   **You fail to follow-up**

      Although you may have your terms and conditions documented, if an invoice is outstanding do you follow-up?

Again, automation and outsourcing can assist here, but the bottom line is when an invoice is overdue, reminders need to be issued, calls need to be made, and further work should stop.

If that fails to work, debt recovery might be your next port of call.

5.   You think you can overlook it

Yes, following up takes work and it does involve treating customers as a customer rather than a friend, but if you think you can overlook overdue invoices, you are sadly mistaken.

The reality is, things in business can rapidly change, and no small or medium business can afford to work for free.

So my question to you is this...what will you do right now to change your mindset and address the systems and procedures that mean your business currently works part-time as a charity undertaking work for free?

Six strategies for dealing with business overwhelm

Feeling a little edgy, anxious or stressed? Welcome to 'business', some would say. But while the feeling of 'overwhelm' might be common, the truth is it doesn't have to be the case.

In simple terms the feeling of overwhelm relates to having too much to do in too little time. It's a position that blinds business operators to future opportunity and the goals they wish to achieve.

So here's a little expert insight into recognising overwhelm and the strategies required to take back the business reins.

Strategy one - break it down

Overwhelm occurs when we have too many thoughts

competing within our mind, and the first step to tackling it is to break down an issue or task into manageable chunks.

Divide tasks into milestones that can be accomplished within a realistic time and write them down in the order each segment will be completed, with a deadline set.

This frees your mind to move onto other matters.

Strategy two - Account for your time

Part of strategy one involves having a good knowledge of exactly how long tasks actually take, and the truth is many business owners fail to adequately account for their time, setting unrealistic expectations of how long things take to do.

To understand where your time is spent, keep a diary that tracks your time precisely for a week. It will reveal a host of intriguing things, like the hour you allocate for invoicing actually takes two by the time you PDF and send items out.

Strategy three - Ensure your price reflects the workload

Now you have a good idea of how long each task takes, does the price you're charging adequately cover your time and effort? Does it account for the extra items involved in a job like phone calls, emails, final checks and invoices. Does it cover the fact additional staff may be required to do the job you do?

If it doesn't you need to a) re-evaluate your pricing, b) streamline tasks or c) both.

Strategy four - Look to simplify tasks

Modern technology means there are a host of business tools available to simplify common tasks, so look for assistance that may suit you. Yes, learning how to use it may take time in the beginning but it could greatly ease your workload in the future.

And it's not just technological areas that could use

simplification, are your internal business procedures as efficient as they could be?

Strategy five - Delegate/outsource tasks

What tasks are there within your business that other people could easily and efficiently do? Is it time to engage a bookkeeper for an hour a week? Could you outsource something like website administration? Or could existing staff take on an additional responsibility?

Strategy six - Practise this tiny word...

"No" - It's one of the most powerful words in the English language, requiring just one syllable and two tiny letters, but so many of us struggle to use it when required.

Sometimes business is about saying no - no to a client who takes up too much of your time. No to a job that will increase your workload too much, or no to jobs where too much is required for too little reward.

And guess what? By saying "no" you're saying "yes" to better service for your other clients, "yes" to less stress, and "yes" to earning what you deserve.

Strategy seven - Keep the end goal in mind

Throughout all areas in business keep the ultimate goals you wish to achieve in mind. Then, when it comes to taking on jobs or completing tasks, run them through the mental filter of your goals.

For example you might ask yourself:

- ◆ Will this job help my business expand?
- ◆ Will this task get me closer to more income?
- ◆ Could my time be better spent on some other element of business?

This allows you to set the most important priorities in the order in which they need to be achieved.

How you feel about your business is critical to the success you're likely to achieve. If you're floundering about feeling overwhelmed day-to-day, the likelihood is you're not looking to your future.

The key is to address the issues that have you feeling overwhelmed, seek the assistance you require and have the strategies you need that allow you to see the wood for the trees.

Chapter 11 - Mitigating Risk

Just like any major financial decision in life, being in business comes with its own level of risk.

Depending on what sort of business you run, where your business is in its journey or your attitude towards entrepreneurship, some business owners may also have a greater appetite for risk than others.

In this chapter we'll take a look at risk and the strategies you can use to mitigate your exposure.

Understanding business risk

Every business has risks attached to it and they come in different forms.

There are the risks associated with strategy, such as new products and growth phases, the risks to your business location such as natural disasters, and human risks including staff selection and habits.

While those risks might be present, they can also be managed, which involves identifying the risk and developing strategies to mitigate it.

So let's look at the different types of business risks that might need to be addressed.

What is business risk?

By definition, business risk is any factor that might threaten an enterprise's ability to achieve its financial goals.

In other words, it is anything that will lower a business' profits or cause it to fail. And this risk can come in many forms.

Types of business risk

Business risk can come down to strategy, operations, or compliance, with experts identifying four common types of risk that need to be identified in any business.

Strategic risk

Strategic risk is all about whether the business has its finger on the pulse of what their customer needs and wants.

And this type of risk can occur at any time. For example, what happens if the product you produce suddenly falls out of favour, or the new line of services you offer doesn't attract the attention you anticipated?

Operational risk

Operational risk is about the systems and procedures within a business. It's part workplace health and safety and also general operations, including cybersecurity.

For example, what happens if machinery breaks down and

orders can't be fulfilled, or if someone gets sick and cannot complete required tasks? It's also about mitigating workplace accidents.

Compliance risk

Compliance risk is arguably one of the easiest to manage. It's about ensuring your business dots all the Is and crosses all the Ts of business, including registering your business name, paying required taxes, ensuring staff are properly accredited and licensed, and that your staff wages and entitlements are being accounted for and paid correctly.

Financial risk

Financial risk is pure economics. It relates to knowing your bottom line, effectively managing cashflow and ensuring you can meet any loan or rent payments, along with wages and other costs.

Risk causes

Behind each type of risk, there are likely to be three common causes – human behaviour, natural disaster, and economic causes.

So let's expand further...

Human behaviour

Human causes of risk are one of the trickiest to navigate. It can relate to anything from staff drug and alcohol abuse, to strikes, poor work performance, error, and mismanagement.

Natural disaster

This cause of risk relates to events that are challenging to foresee, such as floods, fire, cyclones, and yes, even global pandemics.

Economic causes

Economic risks tend to happen outside a business, but impact it directly. Whether that's rising interest rates, inflation, increased material prices, or increased labour costs.

Areas to look at

If you're looking to drill down into your business' risk factors, there are five different areas that are worth considering.

Physical risks

What are the physical risks that are associated with your business or industry? These include risks to staff or your business premises due to the way your business operates.

For example, hazardous materials are a physical risk in some businesses, while plant and equipment might be a risk in others.

This risk is managed through policies and procedures, along with comprehensive Workplace Health and Safety policies.

Locational risks

Locational risks are anything that might affect your business due to its location, such as natural disasters.

Is there a potential for your business to be impacted by flooding, fire, bushfire, cyclones or other naturally occurring events?

Locational risks are managed through insurance and emergency management planning, which we will come to shortly.

Human risks

What could possibly go other than right due to the people working in your business?

Do you have policies and procedures, Workplace Health and Safety guidelines, or rules about expected behaviour to manage the risk of error or negligence within your operation?

This type of risk is also mitigated through good hiring practices, management, disciplinary policies, and business culture.

Technology risks

Whether it's cybersecurity, payment processing, a blackout, or the technology and software that allows your business to function, every business owner should have a fall-back plan for what happens if their technology is compromised or fails.

Technology risks are best managed through policy and procedure, contingency planning, and education.

Strategic risks

In many ways strategic risks are part and parcel of business. After all, even starting an enterprise is a strategic risk, as is introducing a new product or growing your business.

In this instance it's all about understanding your strengths, weaknesses, opportunities and threats along with your personal risk tolerance.

Strategic risk is managed through business planning, goal setting, and KPIs.

Necessary versus unnecessary risk

As we've just highlighted, every business has an element of risk, some of which is necessary. For example, if you don't take calculated risk, then your business will never grow.

However, other risk is unnecessary and can be planned for. So let's now look at risk mitigation tools like Emergency Management Plans and policies and procedures that help curb unnecessary risk.

Mitigating risk

In business we talk about planning all the time – planning for growth, planning for new staff, planning for improvement. But what about when things go really, really wrong and it's beyond our control?

As history indicates, businesses can be affected by circumstances they never anticipated like fires, floods, droughts and electricity outages.

In these instances, it's about planning for the very worst with an Emergency Management and Recovery plan, and it's something every business should have.

This is how emergency plans work and the security they bring...

The plan

Emergency management and recovery plans involve identifying the risks to your business, the strengths and weaknesses within it and planning what happens if something goes wrong.

Often the impact of one disaster would be similar to another.

For example a flood may damage your information systems, and a robbery or fire would be likely to do the same. So planning is not about saying what you would do in the case of a fire, it's about knowing what happens if your vital technology is wiped out.

Planning for this scenario enables you to have a course of action for your business and staff, to mitigate this risk, and find alternative ways to service your clientele.

The key elements of the plan involve:

Identifying a potential risk – Such as power loss, IT failure, produce or stock loss, your office becoming uninhabitable etc and what these things would do to your business.

Assessing its likely impact – Rate the effect this would have on your business: high, medium or low impact.

Rating how likely that risk is – Is it highly likely, likely, unlikely or highly unlikely that this situation could occur?

Creating a mitigation strategy - This involves devising and employing procedures to lessen the likelihood of your business being affected. For example: backing up data and storing it off-site, investing in a generator, or training a number of staff in key areas of the business so no one person is indispensable.

Contingency plan – This section is about outlining and educating staff about what happens if your business is affected. For example, if you rely on refrigeration for your business products and the power fails, your contingency plan will note: where the generator is located, how it works, how long you have until produce starts to spoil, who is responsible for ensuring the generator is in working order, how much fuel it will require etc.

You should also include all your insurance information in your plan including contact people, policy numbers and information about what is covered.

The benefits of risk planning

Having an Emergency Management and Recovery Plan allows you to identify risks and lessen the likelihood of impact, and also allows you to look at potential weaknesses within your business and operating systems.

It enables you to determine the critical elements of your business that you cannot do without and train your staff accordingly.

Should the worst occur, you have a strategy to move forward and recover as swiftly as possible.

Meanwhile, your business' policies and procedures play an important role in mitigating risk.

As mentioned in Chapter 6, policies and procedures should be applied at every point in the business where something can go other than right. As a result they reduce the likelihood that something might go wrong.

As mentioned in Chapter 6 policies and procedures should be applied at every point in the business where a somewhat death could exist if you fail they redirect the like when that something might go wrong.

Chapter 12 - Growth

The five stages of business growth

In the heady world of small business your average tyre repair shop and software start-up may seem light years apart.

But according to a seminal study by Harvard Business Review[7] they're not as different as you think with all small businesses working through the same five stages of business growth, and the challenges each presents.

So let's take a look at the five stages of business growth and how you can identify your path to success.

Existence

If you're reading this as a business owner who started up themselves, chances are 'you've been there and done that'.

This is the phase of business where the enthusiastic

---

[7] https://hbr.org/1983/05/the-five-stages-of-small-business-growth

entrepreneur does everything themselves, perhaps with the assistance of a couple of staff who answer directly to them.

The focus at this stage is customers; how to get them, what to offer them and how to keep them.

It's about creating a viable income stream, with many businesses failing after they exhaust their initial capital.

Survival

Once you've proven your existence, a business is in survival stage, and it's a place where many stay.

This is a critical time for business where they can begin to generate revenue or languish at just above the break-even point using the owner's energy and direction for a minimal return.

The important questions at this time are:

- In the short term can we generate enough return to break even and cover the costs of equipment repair?
- Can we generate enough revenue to fund growth into something viable?

Success

If you've reached success stage, chances are you're enjoying a solid return for your efforts but now there is a vital decision to be made.

Do you sit back and enjoy the income you've built or do you use your revenue as a platform for further growth?

At this point income should be fairly healthy and an owner can choose to step away from the business utilising the resources of staff to enjoy the income and lifestyle return, they can sell their business for a fair profit, or consolidate their resources and grow.

If the latter is the path you choose, planning is imperative. The business will need to have enough cash and expert staff to handle future needs, while systems will need to be implemented that cater to your future direction.

Take-off

At this point delegation and cash are the key focus areas. The business will be evolving at a rapid rate and chances are you may have incurred debt to take it to the next phase.

There will also be significant changes to how an owner operates amid an altered business structure, where the organisation is often departmentalised and decentralised. Key systems and procedures will be refined during this period, often overseen by managers.

The owner may still be intrinsically involved in the company but will be separate from day-to-day operations, and may have opted to employ a company head to lead the growing enterprise.

Maturity

At maturity a company will be stable, proven and experienced. It will have certain power and recognition in the market, but will not be without its challenges.

The focus now is on maintaining position with an eye on competition, developing technology and continued market share, where innovation and diversity will continue to play key roles.

This is a point where many businesses stagnate, relying on their past instead of recognising future opportunity. If a company can maintain its entrepreneurial spirit, flair and hunger while enjoying its strong market position it will have the best chance of prolonged success.

Planning

Throughout the five cycles of business, planning is key. In the early stages that includes strategies to attract and retain customers, and further plans for investment and growth. Later it will focus on the implementation of systems and procedures.

Where to from here?

Identifying growth and movement in your business

One of the greatest challenges for any business owner is to take a big picture approach.

With demanding schedules, competing needs and the daily routine of working in your business it can be hard to step out of the management role and see the wood for the trees, to ask and effectively answer that all important question; where to from here?

Identifying growth and movement in your business is critical to answering that question.

So let's consider what you need to ask to identify growth and movement in your business?

What works now?

You know when something's working – the balance sheet looks good, your customers are happy...but what are the exact ingredients that are underpinning your success?

Take a good hard look at your business to get to the root of the elements that work well. This includes analysing your product lines or business features that have people coming back for more.

It's also about identifying the extraneous items that may be holding you back – whether that's staffing, over-stocking or expense.

What will work in the future?

Determining what works now helps you predict what's likely to work in the future.

Depending on your circumstances, you might wish to expand your product lines, implement systems and procedures, or network with the right customers to cement a prime position in your business niche.

At this stage it's also important to find ways to identify emerging trends, whether that's through research, or expert insight.

Then you need to look for tools that allow you to test the market and help you carve out a natural path of expansion.

What to do next?

Whether it's raising capital, finding suppliers or implementing a media plan, it's important to map out then plan where you want to go.

Once you've deciphered what works, what doesn't, and what looks likely to work in the future, you are in a position to set your goals, plan accordingly and then measure your progress.

The four choices of business growth

Few businesses grow without a commitment to doing so, and it's a process that takes thought, management and planning. Most importantly it's a choice and a mindset.

If you're considering taking your business to the next level, here are the four strategies famously outlined in the Ansoff matrix[8] to 'make it so'.

More of the same, to the same people (market penetration)

Probably one of the least risky options, this is about market penetration.

It relies on marketing your product for more regular use by existing customers, and/or reaching more customers in the

[8] https://en.wikipedia.org/wiki/Ansoff_Matrix

196

same market. It tends to involve aggressive promotion to reach a higher sales volume.

It can be achieved by:

- Price decrease
- Increased promotion and distribution
- Acquisition of a competitor
- Product refinement

More of the same, to new people (market development)

The next option is to broaden your horizons, to take your existing product and seek out new markets, whether that's going national, international or taking your product or service from domestic to commercial application.

It usually relies on a unique product or service, but the benefits include:

- Economies of scale in production
- Previous experience

Different services or products to the same people (product development)

Another option with reduced risk, this involves offering similar or complementary products to your existing customer base.

It can involve:

- Creation of your own new products/services
- Obtaining the rights to market someone else's new product
- The purchase of other people's products and rebranding them in your own name
- Joint development of a new product in conjunction with another business

New items and services to new markets and customers (diversification)

This final strategy probably presents the greatest risk, as it involves both market and product development. But when tied in with a solid business plan, this option can lead to real revenue and growth.

This is particularly the case if you have a bi-product of your existing manufacturing process that can be marketed effectively.

A prime example may be a sugar mill or factory that can create electricity during their refinement process which can be sold back to the grid, or who sells their waste as fertiliser.

Questions to ask yourself

Regardless of which growth option may interest you, there are a series of questions to pose first.

They include:

Are you interested in growth or revenue? – Because if it's purely the latter then there are other ways to achieve your aim, including increasing your profitability by plugging sales leaks or raising prices.

Are you committed? – Growth takes commitment, planning and more often than not, investment. Like starting a business, you have to be ready for the ride.

Do you have a plan? – No growth should be undertaken without proper planning and an assessment of the risks involved.

Have you secured your existing business? – If you do decide to go ahead, ensure your existing business is secure first – that you have dotted the 'Is' and crossed the 'Ts' with ownership of your intellectual property and assets.

The growth mindset

Regardless of where you are in the five stages of business, taking an enterprise to the next level involves embracing a growth mindset.

This is the frame of thinking that sees you welcome and seek opportunity rather than fearing competition and change.

So let's wander the corridors of the entrepreneurial mind and investigate how to develop a growth mindset in business.

Growth versus fixed mindset

In business, the theory of growth versus fixed mindset is based broadly on the research of psychologist Carol Dweck.

In the Harvard Business Review[9], she explains: A growth mindset sees individuals believe their talents can be developed through hard work, good strategies, and input from others, while a fixed mindset sees people believe their talents are innate gifts.

Dweck argues those with a growth mindset tend to achieve more than those with a fixed mindset "because they worry less about looking smart and they put more energy into learning".

She further notes there is no such thing as a pure growth or fixed mindset, individuals tend to have a mix of both. But when you can foster a growth mindset by recognising the triggers that inhibit growth, you have a better chance of prolonged success.

"When we face challenges, receive criticism, or fare poorly compared with others, we can easily fall into insecurity or defensiveness, a response that inhibits growth...To remain in a growth zone, we must identify and work with these triggers."

So how does this play out in business?

---

[9] https://hbr.org/2016/01/what-having-a-growth-mindset-actually-means

The growth mindset in business

In business, a growth mindset can play out across an organisation. From a leadership perspective a growth mindset will see you:

- Understand threats but embrace opportunity
- Look to the next phase
- Learn from business mistakes
- Foster a culture of learning in your leaders and your staff
- Welcome challenge
- Look to innovate
- Have a clear vision of where you wish to be

Conversely, a fixed mindset would see you:

- Looking to the past
- Fearing competition
- Blaming failure on circumstance or industry trend
- Giving up easily or being paralysed by a set back or defeat

So how do you foster this growth mindset in yourself and your business?

The mechanics of a business growth mindset: Vision and Mission

Your Vision and Mission are a great starting point for embracing the growth mindset.

When you clearly document what your company is about, you not only tell your staff and customers what you stand for, you have the mechanism to measure opportunity and say yes or no.

This Vision and Mission should always be viewed as far more

than words. They mean little if they're just pretty sentences on paper without the business philosophy and practice to back them up.

Innovation and learning

How well does your business understand the current marketplace and the present strengths, opportunities, weaknesses and threats?

It's not just about knowing them but having a culture of learning and innovation that allows you to act in response.

How do you gauge the mistakes you have made and what have you and your staff learnt from them?

By understanding and learning from opportunities, threats and mistakes, your business has the tools and insight to innovate and move forward.

Planning - the long game

Planning is imperative to a growth business mindset – not just in the short-term but with a long-term vision of where you want to be.

This planning allows you to innovate, make decisions with clarity and understand the skills or tools your business requires.

A sustainable, repeatable model

If your business is truly committed to growth, part of the planning and assessment involves looking to create a sustainable, repeatable business model.

This requires an understanding of what works and what doesn't, what resources and skills are essential and having the mechanisms to repeat them on a larger scale.

It includes systems, procedures, and a clear understanding of your market along with your business opportunity.

Decisive thinking

Indecision is crippling for any business, leaving it in limbo. Use your Vision, Mission and plan to gauge whether a decision suits your customer and ethos, then say yes or no quickly, and take the required action swiftly.

Delaying a decision equates to fear, value extraction, a lack of direction and absence of quality.

If it turns out to be the wrong decision, take the opportunity to learn. If it turns out to be a good decision, you have reached your destination all the sooner.

Key takeaway

A growth mindset is something that a business and the business owner should actively espouse. It is not a phrase or a buzzword, but a frame of thinking that grants business the room to learn, innovate and ultimately grow.

It is a process, not a destination, but used effectively it furnishes business and operators with the tools and insight to embrace change, seize opportunity, and ultimately thrive.

Five things you need to have in place for business growth

Business growth is often the biggest priority for every business operator. After all, growth equals more revenue, right? Well yes, but only if you have the correct structure in place before you take the next step.

So, let's examine the five things you need to have in place before your business can grow...

A plan

Growth without planning is like setting sail without a map. You need to know where you intend to go and how you plan to get there before you set off.

Otherwise, you put both your vessel and crew at risk of running aground.

Planning for growth involves knowing exactly where you are now, where you intend to be and charting a very clear course of how you intend to get there.

People

Truth be told, there are two ways you can embrace growth when it comes to staffing. You can build it and hope the right staff will come, or you can have the right people in place and expand using their skill.

The latter often works far better than the former when it comes to key moments of business growth. With the right staff already in place, you can expand at speed in the knowledge quality and service will be maintained.

Systems and procedures

They may not be glamourous, but systems and procedures set you up for the scalable, repeatable success that drives business growth.

Basically the 'how to', 'when to' and 'who by' that creates the inner workings of your business, systems and procedures improve a whole host of areas, including training, efficiency and staff productivity.

A grasp on your numbers

Your numbers tell detailed stories about your business, including your strengths, weaknesses, opportunities and threats.

Only when you understand exactly where you are now in cold hard numerical terms, can you begin to plan for where you intend to go in the form of KPIs and targets.

In turn, consistent evaluation of your numbers will tell you whether your growth strategy is working or whether something needs revision.

A growth mindset

A growth mindset is the frame of thinking that sees you welcome and seek opportunity rather than fearing competition and change.

As a business, it allows you to:

- Understand threats but embrace opportunity
- Look to the next phase
- Learn from business mistakes
- Foster a culture of learning in your leaders and your staff
- Welcome challenge
- Look to innovate
- Have a clear vision of where you wish to be

Questions every business owner should consistently ask

Throughout the life of a business enterprise owners should regularly ask questions, both of themselves and their business. Why? Because when we ask questions, we begin to better understand our business, our customer and ourselves, along with the opportunities for growth.

Here are five of the top questions every business operator should regularly ask.

What business do I want to be in?

If you have an established business this might sound like a strange question, but it's an important one that is worth revisiting regularly.

Sometimes the business we operate isn't the business we expected to be in at all, or the item we are actually selling is different to what we believe.

For example, the day-to-day life of a real estate agency might involve selling houses but the core proposition of that operation is actually trust.

So ask yourself, what business do you want to be in? Is it trust, convenience, time saving, aspiration, or lifestyle – is it something else?

When you know what business you are in, it helps you better understand the business proposition you are marketing, and assists in determining the products or services that fit that bill.

It also allows you to better embrace the right staff to represent your business and it helps answer the next question, which is...

Where to from here?

If you're always looking in the rearview mirror, you don't have full focus on the road ahead, which is why business owners should frequently ask themselves: where to from here?

Where do I want to be in 12 months, five years and a decade? How will my business service those plans, and what do I need to do right now to achieve those goals?

Business planning (considering where to from here) is essential throughout the life of an operation – regardless of whether you're in your first year of business or your fortieth.

Importantly, this question should take in your current business landscape, factoring in strengths, weaknesses, opportunities and threats.

Is there a better way?

Whether it's adopting technology, employing additional staff or running your business under management, asking yourself whether there's a better way of doing business allows you to evaluate how you do business now and seek improvements for your products, your services and your bottom line.

It ensures you're moving with the times and meeting your goals, by revisiting your systems, procedures and the day-to-day operation of your business.

How are we doing?

This is a question to put to your customers, and it's one that business owners fail to ask often enough.

By seeking feedback from your clientele, you can identify areas in a business which fail to live up to expectation, where improvements can be made, and where product lines or services can potentially be developed.

Am I happy?

A business should facilitate your lifestyle not dictate it, which begs the question: are you happy?

Do you find joy in your work, does it give you pride, does it provide the lifestyle you hoped for and does it meet the personal goals you set?

If the answer is no, that's a clear sign you need to:

A. Re-evaluate your business, look at the bottom line and consider how it services your lifestyle

B. Reconsider your business plan and look at how it can get you where you want to be

C. Revisit why you entered business in the first place, and look at whether it's still a challenge you're happy and enthused to meet. If not, what needs to change?

The value of questions

By regularly questioning the achievements of business, your role within it, and its role within your greater goals in life, you better understand what motivates and drives you, and the steps we need to take in order to succeed.

Questioning keeps business relevant and ensures business owners remain invested in their enterprise, because as Eugene Ionesco once said: "It is not the answer that enlightens, but the question".

Chapter 13 - The measure of success

We can talk about goals, KPIs, and growth as much as we like, but the true measure of business is drawn from a far greater perspective:

- ◆ **Is your business what you intended it to be?**
- ◆ **Does your business meet your lifestyle needs and goals?**

After all, these are the two primary reasons that people enter business, to achieve an ambition and to gain financial security that facilitates their lifestyle.

From that overarching position, we then work backwards to measure the success of our business in the following areas:

Business financial statements

Measuring your business' success starts with the cold hard basics of how much money it is bringing in, making the first port of call your business financial statements.

These tell you what exactly is coming in, what's going out, and how far above or below break-even point your business is.

The three main statements to look at here are your:

- **Income statement** – which looks at profitability.
- **Balance sheet** – which determines your business health and what you owe and own.
- **Cashflow statement** – Which indicates how much liquidity your business actually has.

Customer satisfaction

Beyond the cold hard cash, measuring success is also about determining how your customers feel about your business.

The most important thing to ascertain here is whether they are satisfied and likely to buy from you again.

The reality is, satisfied customers who are willing to either use your business again or refer you to other customers are a core element of business success. Further answers can also be found in the general numbers of your business, including repeat versus new clientele.

New clientele

When you know how many new clients you average each month or each quarter, you have the opportunity to predict growth.

This also allows you to gauge how effective things like your marketing strategy are. For example, if your business attracts few new clients each quarter, it's likely your marketing isn't reaching your ideal client where they 'hang out'.

Performance reviews and staff feedback

Client satisfaction and new client numbers tell you how your business is viewed from the outside, but what about the internal workings and culture of your enterprise?

It's no secret, happy staff result in happier customers, so it's equally important to understand how staff feel about your business.

You can gauge this by actively seeking staff feedback, having an open-door policy, and simply by asking staff about potential areas of business improvement during their annual performance review.

Market trends and SWOT

No business operates in isolation. It is impacted by factors like market forces, competition, innovation and more.

To truly understand your business' position, you should view it within the context of that market, regularly undertaking exercises like listing your strengths, weaknesses, opportunities and threats (SWOT) to see how it's performing right now, in the current conditions.

Regularly assessing your SWOT also allows you to understand both future opportunities and liabilities.

Your own expectation

Every business owner has expectations of their business, and whether your enterprise meets (or is on track to meet) those aims is a definite measure of its success.

As a business owner you should regularly ask yourself:

- Am I where I want to be?
- Is this what I wanted?
- Does my business make me happy?
- Does it serve the purpose I intended it to in my life (financial, work/life balance, lifestyle?)

After all, the true measure of business success is the satisfaction it affords you, and the personal goals it allows you to attain.

Maintaining your vision

As exciting as the early days of business might be, maintaining your enthusiasm, drive and commitment in the long-term can occasionally prove challenging during the inevitable highs and lows of any enterprise.

So how do you set about maintaining your vision and keep the big front of mind?

Know your why

There are different reasons for being in business and different drivers behind the service or products you provide.

Throughout the life of your business, you need to be acutely aware of your why. Your why drives your business Vision as the personal and professional motivation for getting out of bed each morning and throwing the doors of your business open to customers.

Share your Vision

The Vision you have for your business should be front of mind for you, your staff and your customers.

Write it large, refer to it often and share it frequently. Use it to determine every decision you make for your business, and ensure your staff or management team refer to it too.

Embrace change

One thing is certain in life, and that's change. Throughout your business journey, this is something you will need to embrace.

Not only is change a constant, it is something you need to proactively anticipate in business, looking at your strengths, opportunities, weaknesses and threats.

Also it's important to appreciate, while the situation around you may change, your Vision need not. This is the tether that anchors your business through every storm and every challenge along the way.

Understand the journey

Every business involves a journey. There will be times when success comes easily and times when things can be tough.

Every challenge you encounter along the way is an opportunity for learning and growth.

While that initial passion and drive that propelled you in the early stages of your business may wane over the years, you can revive it by seeking opportunity, looking at areas of growth and ensuring your personal and professional 'why' remains front of mind.

Plan your work, work your plan

Business success is all about planning, and that's not just limited to your actual business plan.

When you plan exactly what you will achieve each day and how you will go about it, you set yourself up to achieve all the micro-steps that lead to you achieving your Vision.

Creating action through accountability

It's all very well to set goals and have a plan, but how do you ensure you maintain the action required to achieve your Vision?

Well, that comes down to holding yourself and your team accountable.

With that in mind, here are the top tips on creating accountability in your business...

Have an accurate and achievable Vision

A business Vision is the first stage of planning what you hope to achieve for your business. As such, that vision should accurately reflect where you want to go, but most importantly it should be achievable.

It's all very well to aspire to lofty ideals, but these should be contained in your Mission, while your Vision is all about what you can feasibly do right now and into the immediate future.

Have a plan

Your business plan creates the roadmap to achieve that Vision, and includes the steps you need to reach along the way.

That plan should be clear, communicated to your team and regularly revised to reflect what you have already achieved and the way your business changes over time.

Set milestones

With your Vision and plan as the framework, creating action then involves deciphering the milestones (goals) you need to reach as part of your business' immediate journey.

These milestones should be clear, and have a deadline, which must be achieved.

Create ownership

Meeting milestones involves assigning responsibility for set tasks - whether that's the roll out of a new product, achieving a KPI, or delivering an outcome within a set timeframe.

To achieve action, ensure you assign ownership to members of your team. Include clear deliverables, deadlines, and write it down as part of their job description or the project brief.

Have a process and procedure

To achieve consistent action, create processes and procedures that allow for consistency.

These processes and procedures take the guesswork out of completing tasks and also create efficiency within a business that allows for repeatable, scalable success.

Seek mentors

If you are a business leader looking to hold yourself accountable, seek a mentor or multiple mentors who will help you maintain the momentum you require.

These people might be personal mentors, professional mentors, or even business coaches, but their role is to help you define your goals, and help you meet them by being an exterior influence to whom you feel accountable.

Be consistent

Consistent activity creates results over time. In other words it's about making activity a habit.

Ensure you set yourself up for success by writing down your goal and creating regular timeframes to work towards it - whether that's a small activity daily, or a larger activity weekly.

Create rewards

Too often we race towards a major goal, without marking the small milestones along the way. But, by rewarding yourself for activities that lead to your ultimate destination, you create a winning culture where you recognise success.

When you create milestones, set rewards that act as an incentive to achieve them.

Be in the moment

As much as you might be working towards a set destination, it's important to remain in the moment and acknowledge how far you have already come.

Being in the moment allows you to better understand your business, its goals and why they continue to matter.

Manage your time

Time management is critical when it comes to achieving tasks and creating action.

Track your time to see where it's spent, outsource what you need to and schedule time to work on your goals.

Accountability isn't easy

Creating accountability is about recognising that your goals are important. However, that's not to say it's easy.

Often small day-to-day responsibilities and distractions can get in the way of taking the actions that you want to in order to move your business forward.

That's why it pays to see accountability as important and look at it as a skill that needs to be mastered.

When you hold yourself and your team accountable for activities that progress your business vision, you are far more likely to get where you want to go.

Continuous measuring

One of the best ways of holding yourself accountable and also tracking the activity in your business is through continuous measuring.

This allows you to see what your business has achieved and also helps you set goals then plan for the future.

Through continuous measuring of key figures, you can see where you have come from and create the milestones you and your team are accountable to.

Small steps big results

Small steps inevitably lead to big results in business. Like a habit these activities build on themselves over time, bringing you closer and closer to achieving your ultimate goal.

Reflecting on achievement

Your goals - What goals did you set, which ones did you meet?

If you set goals and met all, chances are you have learned that you can achieve what you set out to do and next year you can aim higher.

If you set goals, but met some, you have the opportunity to look at why these goals were harder to achieve than expected and re-frame them for the year ahead, if they remain a priority.

Your plan - Did you follow it?

In addition to your goals, both personally and professionally, you probably had a plan for the year that was.

Did you follow it? Did you tick off the items on your to-do list? Are you closer to where you expected to be?

If so, well done. What did you learn during that endeavour? Was the plan too simple, could it be more challenging? Was it a challenge that you met despite the odds and next year you can enjoy the fruits of your labour, with greater challenges ahead.

Did you set a plan but not follow it? If so, why did it prove too hard or irrelevant? There are valuable lessons to be learned in planning here, and there's the potential to implement small milestones that may allow you to reach your goals better next year.

Your customer - Did you understand them?

Your customer can change from year to year in a business. How well did you know yours over the past year?

If you clearly knew them and understood them, chances are selling to them was almost incidental.

But if you found selling a challenge, you may have been preaching to the wrong choir, and should look to redefine your customer going forward.

Your numbers - Did you know them?

Did you know and understand your numbers in the past year? Because they tell a story in business.

Your numbers illustrate key facts like how many people frequented your business, how many potential clients your staff spoke to then how many purchased from you.

They then illustrate the profit you enjoyed or areas which were lacking.

If you found your numbers something to fear or hard to deal with, there's a lesson there that within them is something you don't wish to address.

If you did know your numbers they would have revealed a wealth of detailed insight about your business.

Your business, your life - Did your business serve your lifestyle

Finally, was your business something you remained passionate about? Or was it overwhelming, a burden and too time consuming?

If the latter three are true, now is the time to reposition - to clearly define the purpose that your business serves and how it fits with the life you want.

By learning from the business lessons of the past, you have the potential to rethink, redefine and re-embrace what you want both personally and professionally in the future.

Learning from both the good and the bad, the wins and the losses allows us to grow.

Business is a Conversation

At the start, the middle and the end of the day, business is a conversation, just a conversation.

Having the right conversation is the difference between struggling and having a business that can give you all you thought you wanted when you commenced the entrepreneurial journey.

What makes a good business conversation?

- Identify a person is interested in what you offer
- Discover they are ready to discuss / approach the subject
- Identify their need
- Arrive at them wanting it in the manner you deliver it
- Show them what you deliver and how you deliver it
- Arrive at a mutually beneficial outcome

Three things provide the foundations that let you have that conversation with your ideal customer over and over and over again.

1. Values
2. Mission
3. Vision

When you know these and align all else with these, having that conversation is uncomplicated and painless.

Here's to better business.

BOOK A DISCOVERY CALL WITH CLIVE

As a Business Strategist, the correct mindset is the foundation to both my and and my clients' success. If you would like my assistance in creating a productive mindset, armed with the tools to achieve business growth and longevity, our journey starts with a discovery call where we explore where you are now and where you want to go.

Clive's Suite of Products - cliveenever.com.au/shop
Join The Strategy Circle - cliveenever.com.au/the-strategy-circle
Coaching Session with Clive - cliveenever.com.au/booking-calendar
Contact Clive - cliveenever.com.au/contact-clive

Follow Clive:

Website - cliveenever.com.au
Facebook - facebook.com/CliveEneverBusiness
Twitter - twitter.com/cliveenever
Linkedin - linkedin/in/cliveenever
Instagram - instagram.com/cliveenever

www.ingramcontent.com/pod-product-compliance
Lightning Source LLC
Chambersburg PA
CBHW071207210326
41597CB00016B/1703